WHEN

WHEN IN SPAIN

A holidaymaker's guide to the language and the country

Derek Utley

Producers
Bernard Adams
Alan Wilding

BBC BOOKS

This book accompanies the BBC Television series
When in Spain first broadcast on BBC 1 from April
1987 (produced by Bernard Adams) and the Radio
series of the same name first broadcast on Radio 4
VHF from April 1987 (produced by Alan Wilding)

Published to accompany a series of programmes
prepared in consultation with the BBC Educational
Broadcasting Council

Acknowledgement is due to the following:
BERNARD ADAMS pages 32 *bottom right* & 48; BAR-
NABY'S PICTURE LIBRARY pages 57 & 61; J. ALLAN CASH
PHOTOLIBRARY pages 1, 20 *bottom*, 25, 28, 32 *top* &
bottom left, 56 *bottom*, 60, 64 *both*, & 96 *bottom*; LUIS
ESPAÑA pages 24 and 49; JAIME SUAREZ GARCIA pages
17, 20 *top*, 29, 33, 36, 41 & 45; MINISTRY OF TRANSPORT
TOURISM AND COMMUNICATIONS, MADRID page 56 *top*;
PICTUREPOINT pages 13, 16 *bottom*, 65 & 69; ANDREW
SACHS page 44; SPECTRUM COLOUR LIBRARY 37, 73 &
96 *top*; PAUL C. WALDOCK pages 16 *top* & 40; ALAN
WILDING pages 52, 68 & 72.

Cover photography:
CHRIS RIDLEY *portraits;* SPECTRUM COLOUR LIBRARY
background; CHROMACOPY *photocomposite.*

JOHN GILKES maps and diagrams

© The Author and BBC Enterprises Limited 1987
First published 1987

Published by BBC Books a division of BBC Enterprises Ltd,
Woodlands, 80 Wood Lane, London W12 0TT

ISBN 0 563 21284 5

This book is set in 9 on 10½ point Century Schoolbook
Printed in England by Belmont Press, Northampton

CONTENTS

About this book 6

Spain and the Spanish 8

The Language 10

Raciones 1-15

1 Getting a drink 13
2 Getting some basics 17
3 Making yourself known 21
4 What language do you speak? 25
5 Finding your way around 29
6 Trying the tapas 33
7 Shopping for food and drink 37
8 Shopping for gifts 41
9 Getting hotel accommodation 45
10 Pause for a snack 49
11 Being sociable 53
12 Car wise 57
13 Trips and excursions 61
14 Eating out 1 65
15 Eating out 2 69

Grammar with 'L' Plates 74

Useful words 77

Answers 87

Spanish – English vocabulary 92

ABOUT THIS BOOK

- It's for people who are attracted to Spain, and would like to know something about the country, the people and the language.

- It's a pocket book written to help you to make the most of a holiday visit and originates from a BBC tv and radio series: 'When in Spain'.

- It's divided into 15 sections called **raciones** (*portions*). Each of these covers 4 pages and contains:
  useful information about Spain – from the best things to eat and drink, to shopping for souvenirs and going on excursions,
  handy words and phrases to help you start speaking simple Spanish,
  two sections in which you can test your newly-acquired knowledge of Spanish: **tryout** and **quiz**.

- At the back there is a reference section in which you can check up on points of Spanish.

HOW TO USE IT
- Choose a **ración** – they can be taken in any order. Then, read the brief **When in Spain** notes which set the scene for that particular ración.

- Try to learn the handy phrases that will get you speaking simple Spanish straight away. (There's a pronunciation guide on p 10).

- Then read **action** – parts of the real conversations recorded in Spain by actors Andrew Sachs and Miguel Peñaranda for the TV and radio programmes.

- Then look at **replay**, which tells you a bit more about how the language works.

- Have a go at **tryout** and **quiz** and check your results at the back.

'WHEN IN SPAIN' CASSETTE

Apart from this book there's a C90 audio cassette which will give you more help with speaking Spanish. On it Andrew Sachs learns to use the Spanish from each **ración** with the help of Miguel Peñaranda and Cristina Lago.

> **A few hints for 'Saying it in Spanish'**
>
> Don't worry about your accent. Unless you go wildly wrong they'll understand you – and they like foreign accents in Spain!
>
> Have a go even if you don't feel 100% confident – Spaniards really appreciate anyone who tries to speak their language.
>
> It pays to start speaking to Spaniards in Spanish – you're almost bound to find you'll get better service and a warmer welcome wherever you go.

El mundo hispánico – the Hispanic world

SPAIN AND THE SPANISH

WHAT YOU MIGHT KNOW ALREADY
Spain has many wonderful beaches, a perfect climate for all kinds of holidays, superb scenery, and an amazing variety of inexpensive produce, especially fruit and wine. Perhaps most important of all, it has a population which is mostly warm, welcoming and friendly. Not surprisingly, more than six million Britons spend their holidays there each year.

WHAT YOU MIGHT NOT KNOW
- Spain is very big – over twice as big as Britain. Always check the scale of maps before planning a journey, it might be further than you think!

- Spain is one of Europe's most mountainous countries: main roads sometimes have to go round mountain ranges, so journeys might take longer than you thought.

- Spain is not all sunbathing and swimming; inland from the coasts is an immense variety of landscape, from jagged peaks to rolling plains, from forest to arid desert-like areas. Major cities like Barcelona and Madrid contrast richly with medieval villages and fairy-tale castles.

- The climate is varied, and not always fit for sunbathing. The North and North-West get plenty of rainfall; the interior (the Central Meseta or Plateau) is blisteringly hot in summer and bitterly cold in winter; the South (Andalusia) is also very hot in summer, and relatively mild in winter.

...AND ALSO WORTH KNOWING...
- Spain, like Britain, is a monarchy with two Houses of Parliament, but in Spain both are elected.

- It has a population of 37 million (about three quarters of the UK's).

- Since January 1986 Spain has been a member of the EEC (Common Market), as well as of NATO

- Spain is not just a peninsula: the Balearic Isles (Majorca, Menorca and Ibiza are the three biggest) are also part of

Spain, as are the Canary Isles, way down off the coast of Africa. And there are also some small areas across the Straits of Gibraltar in Africa that belong to Spain.

• Gibraltar forms part of the Spanish mainland, yet it still belongs to Britain: a touchy subject for Spaniards.

• Spain (España) used to be called 'The Spains' (Las Españas), because of the enormous differences between the various areas. These differences – of geography, climate, history and language – are still great, and are reflected in the **Autonomías** (Autonomous Local Governments) which have been set up replace the old centralist system of government. Spaniards are very proud of their region and often refer to themselves as, say, Catalan, Basque, Galician as well as Spanish.

Spain and its Regions

THE LANGUAGE

Spanish is spoken not only by Spaniards, but also by nearly 300 million people in the rest of the world, mainly in the countries of Central and South America.

There are some 30 million Spanish speakers in the USA, where experts have predicted it will eventually be more widely spoken than English. At the moment it's third in the world only to Mandarin Chinese and English.

Spanish pronunciation needs a bit of effort with the tongue and throat at first, but holds no real fears for those sound in wind and spirit. In fact Spanish is fairly easy to pronounce because you say the words exactly as they're written.

Many people reckon that Spanish is an easy language to get your teeth into. But there's only one way to find out...

GETTING STARTED
Two things will help you with the **raciones** that follow: a word about pronunciation (below), and a few key phrases that can be useful in any situation (First words p.12).

Letters and sounds
Spanish spelling is much more consistent than English, so the written word is much closer to the spoken. Some letters are pronounced much as they are in English. The following is a rough guide to those letters which might be pronounced differently from English.

- **a**   'a' as in Northern English 'cat'
  adiós (good-bye).

- **e**   'e' as in 'hen'
  encantado (delighted).

- **i**   'ee' as in 'seen'
  vivo (I live)

- **o**   'o' as in 'rob'
  blanco (white)

u	'oo' as in 'pool' **uno** (one)
c	+e/i 'th' as in 'thick'* **Bar**ce**lona; ra**ci**ón** (portion)
c	+any other letter: 'c' as in 'come' **¿Cómo?** (Pardon?) **crema** (cream) calle cuatro
g	+e/i 'ch' as in Scottish 'loch' **ginebra** (gin); **Gerona**
g	+ other letters 'g' as in 'grid' **gracias** (thank you)
h	easy – never pronounced **helado** (ice cream)
j	'ch' as in Scottish 'loch' **Rioja** (wine-producing region)
†**ll**	'y' as in 'yes' **me llamo** (my name is)
†**ñ**	'ni' as in 'onion' **mañana** (tomorrow)
qu	'k' as in 'key' **¿qué?** (what?)
r	'r' is slightly rolled **cerveza** (beer); **Madrid**
rr	rolled more strongly **Correos** (post office) NB when 'r' starts a word it's pronounced like 'rr' **rojo** (red); **ración** (portion)
v	the same as 'b' as in 'bar' **vino** (wine)
x	's' as in 'best' **excelente** (excellent)
y	'y' as in 'yes' (but with a touch of 'j' as in 'jam') **ya** (already)
z	'th' as in 'thick'* **cerveza** (beer), **zapato** (shoe)

---

* In Southern Spain and Spanish-speaking America, the 'th' sound (as in Bar**c**elona) is pronounced 's'.
† In the dictionary, **ll** comes at the end of the entries under **l**, **ch** at the end of the **c's**, and **ñ** after the **n's**.

Saying words

Every word in Spanish has a very clear *stress:* one syllable which is pronounced more emphatically than the other(s). Something similar happens in English when we stress the *al* of *al*phabet. To find out which is the stressed syllable in a word which you see written, take these simple steps:

(i) Does the word have a written accent on it? If so, the letter with the accent (it will always be a vowel) will be stressed. Café; ración; Málaga.

(ii) If there's no written accent, does the word end in a vowel (a e i o u), an n or an s? If so, the stress falls on the next to last syllable: hola; servicios; llaman

(iii) Does the word end in anything else (that is – any consonant except n or s?) If so, the stress falls on the last syllable: Madrid; Benidorm; español.

First words
Try to learn these words before you go any further.

1 Hallo (any time)	**hola**
Good morning	**buenos días**
Good afternoon	**buenas tardes**
Good evening	**buenas noches**

You can also say **hola**, followed by any of the others:
hola, buenas tardes
hola, buenos días

2 Goodbye (any time) **adiós**

You can say **adiós** plus any of the phrases above:
adiós, buenos días
adiós, buenas noches

hasta luego (more casual)

3 Please **por favor**

4 Thank you **gracias**
Thank you very much **muchas gracias**

5 In answer to **gracias** or **muchas gracias** people reply 'don't mention it': **de nada**

GETTING A DRINK

RACIÓN 1

WHEN IN SPAIN …
One of the pleasantest things about being in Spain is sampling the huge range of drinks they have – from various types of coffee and freshly-made fruit juices to beer, wine and spirits. Here's how to order a drink.

- You just name what you want and add 'please'.

un café (a coffee)
un vaso de vino (a glass of wine) } + **por favor**
una cerveza (a beer)

- When you're ready to pay you ask 'How much is it?':

¿Cuánto es?

- After that all you have to do is understand the price. (Numbers on page 82)

Sitges – a bodega

ACTION

Andrew orders a beer.

Barman	**Buenas tardes.**
Andrew	**Una cerveza, por favor.**
Andrew	**Gracias** (when it arrives).

Miguel orders a coke, a beer and a coffee.

Miguel	**Una coca cola, una cerveza y un café, por favor.**
Barman	**Muy bien, muchas gracias.**

Now he orders a black coffee and a glass of brandy.

Barman	**Hola, buenos días. Qué desea el señor?**
Miguel	**Quiero un café y una copa de coñac, por favor.**
Barman	**Vale, en seguida.**

Miguel pays for three drinks he's just had:

Miguel	**¡Pascual!.. ¿Cuánto es?**
Pascual	**Doscientas pesetas, total.**
Miguel	**Doscientas pesetas, gracias.**
Pascual	**Vale, muchas gracias.**

REPLAY

1 When the waiter approaches you, he'll probably say **¿qué desea?** (What would you like?) And when you order he'll probably say **muy bien** or **vale**, which mean 'fine', or **en seguida**, which means 'right away'.

2 'Of' comes into ordering quite a lot – and it's easy: **de**. So a glass of brandy is **una copa *de* coñac** (or simply **una copa**); a glass of wine is **un vaso *de* vino.**

3 'A' and 'one' are the same word in Spanish – or rather the same two words: **un** or **una**. Try to remember which one goes with each word. There's more about this on page 74.

4 'With' is **con**: **café con leche** (white coffee), **té con leche** (tea with milk), **whisky con hielo** (whisky with ice), **ginebra con tónica** (gin and tonic).

5 If you ask for **una cerveza** you'll usually get bottled beer; draught beer is **una caña de cerveza** (¼ litre).

6 **¿cuánto es?**: if you're writing you have to put an upside-down question mark at the start as well as one at the end.

7 optional extra: **Quiero** (I want, I'd like).

PARADOR NACIONAL DE TORDESILLAS

MINIBAR

DENOMINACION DESIGNATION DESIGNATION	Número de Consumiciones	PRECIO UNIDAD	TOTAL PESETAS
Agua sin gas ½			
Agua con gas ½			
Cerveza			
C. Cola			
Refresco naranja			
Refresco limón			
Tónica			
Soda			
Champagne ½			
Champagne ¼			
Zumos varios de frutas			
Frutos secos			
Brandy (coñac)			
Ron			
Ginebra			
Jerez dulce o seco			
Anís			
Vermut			
Pippermint			
Whisky escocés			
Sangría			

Fecha ____ de ____ de 19 ____   TOTAL

Nombre _____ Habitación / Room / Chambre

Firma / Signature

Cargado en Fra. n.° _____

TRYOUT

1 You sit down on the terrace of a café one afternoon. How do you ask the waiter for a draught beer? (Don't forget to say 'Hello').

2 You go into a bar one morning with a friend. You know your friend wants a black coffee, you want a large white. How do you order these? (See page 16)

3 Now it's time for an aperitif; order a glass of white wine for yourself and whisky on the rocks for your friend.

4 After a meal you go to a bar for a glass of brandy and a small, strong white coffee. What do you say?

QUIZ

1 *Four-letter words* Fill in the missing letters in these four-letter words. They're all drinks. What are they?

c a ñ a; c o p a; c a f e; v i n o

2 *Wordbuild* Which drink can be made up from these letters? You can use any of the letters as many times as you like, but you don't *have* to use all of them:

acelmnrvz   cerveza

Where to get a drink

In Spain you can get most types of drinks in most places – whether it's called *un bar, un café, una cafetería, un mesón* (inn), *una bodega* (wine cellar) or even *un pub*.

• Opening times are much more free and easy than in Britain – usually most of the day and well into the night.

• You pay for your drinks when you're ready to leave, and it's normal to leave about a 10% tip.

• If you have your drinks at a table they'll cost more than at the bar – and even more if you have them on the *terraza* outside.

The price of a drink

What's cheap – wine, brandy, sparkling wine (can be half the British price). martini, sangria
What's not so cheap – Scotch, sherry

Coffee in Spain

Black coffee: *un café solo*.

White coffee: *un café con leche* (a coffee with milk) is the breakfast variety. *Un cortado* is a stronger, smaller white coffee, often served in a glass.

If you ask for *un café* they'll normally assume you want *un café solo*.

But they might check ¿*solo, cortado, o con leche?*

Drinks cost a little more on the terraza

Mijas, Costa del Sol

GETTING SOME BASICS

RACIÓN 2

WHEN IN SPAIN ...
You'll find a well-organised chain of tourist offices in Spain. Look for the sign: **Turismo** or **Oficina de Turismo.** They'll give you advice, brochures, lists of restaurants, hotels, fiestas and shows, and street maps. Most of it is free.

- To ask for something, name it and add 'please'.
un plano de Tossa, por favor

- To ask 'Have you got ...?' start with **¿Tiene ...?**

- When buying stamps say where they're for:
cuatro sellos para { **Inglaterra** (England) / **Irlanda** (Ireland) / **Escocia** (Scotland) }

- When people hand you things they often say **aquí tiene** (here is).

Tourist office

ACTION

Newly arrived in Tossa, Andrew – wise man – goes to the Tourist Office to get a plan of the town.

Andrew	**Buenos días.**
Receptionist	**Buenos días, señor.**
Andrew	**Un plano de Tossa de Mar, por favor …**
Receptionist	**Aquí tiene un plano de Tossa**
Andrew	**Muchísimas gracias**

Carmen asks for a map of Elche

Carmen	**Hola, buenos días.**
Empleado	**Buenos días.**
Carmen	**¿Tiene un plano de Elche, por favor?**
Empleado	**Sí, un momento.**

Miguel went to a stationer's for some postcards but was unlucky with the stamps

Miguel	**Hola, buenos días.**
Shopkeeper	**Buenos días.**
Miguel	**¿Tiene postales?**
Shopkeeper	**Sí.** (pointing).
Miguel	**¡Aha! … Una, dos, y tres ¿Cuánto es?**
Shopkeeper	**Cuarenta y cinco**
Miguel	**Muchas gracias. ¿Tiene sellos?**
Shopkeeper	**No, eso en el estanco.***

* see page 20

REPLAY

1 **Un sello** is both 'a stamp' and 'one stamp'. When you want more than one, in Spanish as in English you add an 's': **dos sellos**. If the word ends in a consonant (***a e i o u***), add 'es': **una postal – dos postales**.

2 'For' is **para**

3 You'll need to say the names of the countries you intend to send postcards or letters to, so decide which they are, and try to memorise them. You'll find the countries on page 80.

4 You can't get away from numbers! The thing to remember is that more often than not you need only recognise them when you hear them. Just occasionally you may have to pronounce them. So turn to page 82, listen to the cassette if possible, and practise saying and recognising them.

TRYOUT

1 You're in Benidorm and would like a plan of the town, so you go into the **Oficina de Turismo.** What do you ask for?

2 You've just written a card to a friend in Manchester, and you want to send it off straight away, so you go into an **estanco.** What do you ask for?

3 Then you remember you have a friend on holiday in France, so get a stamp for her card while you're at it.

4 The lady behind the counter gives you two stamps and says: **'Setenta pesetas'.** How much do you give her?

QUIZ

1 *Wordsearch*   All the numbers from one to ten inclusive are contained in this square, except one. Which one? You can move in a straight line in *any* direction (including diagonally) to find the numbers.

```
C U O S E T A
I C S N T R E
N U E V E S I
C A D O I R O
O T R E S H U
T R S D C A O
D O S O N U E
```

2 *'L' Plates*   Only the l's are given in these three words. Can you supply the missing letters to make up words you now know really well?

a _ _ _ _ _ l (might have a view on it)
b _ l _ _ _   (helps you get around a town)
c _ _ l l _   (sticky on the back)

3 *International mix-up*   Sort out the letters to spell the name of a European country. (List on page 80, if you're not sure.)

a **alanrigert**
b **sañepa**
c **naldria**
d **asgel**
e **arincaf**

What is an Estanco?

Estancos are the official state tobacco shops and you recognise them by their special sign outside every one. They also sell postcards, stationery and, of course, stamps, but their main sales are to smokers.

Madrid – estanco

Stamps and the post

You can get stamps at several places:

– at an **estanco**, a tobacconist's shop
– at a **quiosco**, street kiosk, with your postcard
– at the reception desk of your hotel
– at a post office (usually open only 9 till 2 pm)

By the way postcards cost less to send than letters in Spain in the summer. And you can't *always* get stamps in a *quiosco*.

Madrid, Puerta del Sol – quiosco

MAKING YOURSELF KNOWN

RACIÓN 3

WHEN IN SPAIN ...
Spaniards are naturally chatty and, given half a chance, will engage you in conversation. First things first – your name and where you're from.

- How someone will ask your name:

¿Cómo se llama usted (or **¿Cómo te llamas?**)
You answer:

Me llamo { Christine.
Bob Jones.

- How they'll ask 'Where are you from?':

¿De dónde es usted? (or **¿De dónde eres?**)
You answer 'I'm from ...':

Soy de { Alicante.
Manchester

- To say your nationality

soy { inglés/inglesa (English)
escocés/escocesa (Scottish)

ACTION
Andrew gets a lesson from Manuel on how to say his name and nationality.

Me llamo Andrew Sachs.
Soy inglés.

Later, on the beach, he dreams of introducing himself to a lady.

Soy de Inglaterra.

Miguel went to talk to two teachers in a school near Valencia.

Miguel	**¡Hola! ¿cómo se llama usted?**
María	**Me llamo María Pérez.**
Miguel	**¿De dónde es usted?**

María   **Soy de Valencia.**
Miguel   **¿Cómo te llamas?**
Carolina   **Carolina.**
Miguel   **¿Eres valenciana?**
Carolina   **Sí.**

REPLAY

1 Saying your name is pretty easy: **Me llamo ...** but asking somebody else theirs requires a bit more thought. If it's somebody you can be fairly friendly with, say: **¿Cómo te llamas?** But if it's somebody slightly more formal, use: **¿Cómo se llama usted?**
For more ideas on the different words for 'you' see page 76.
2 'Are you...?' can also be said in two ways: **¿Eres ...?** for the 'friendly' way and **¿Es usted ...?** for the more formal approach.
3 The full phrase for 'I am' is **yo soy** but the **yo** is unnecessary and in fact is usually dropped.
4 When it comes to nationality, learn the word for yours (list on page 80). But there's an extra detail to watch: women have an extra letter on the end of the word for their nationality:
Women   **soy española, soy inglesa, soy escocesa** etc.
Men   **soy español, soy inglés, soy escocés** etc.
5 To bounce a question back at someone, use: **¿y usted?** or **¿y tú?** (How about you?)

TRYOUT

1 A person you have seen several times on the beach starts to talk to you: **¿Cómo te llamas?** What do you reply?
2 An elderly gentleman in your hotel starts to talk to you. You'd like to ask him his name; what do you say?
3 A toddler comes up to you in a café. How would you ask her her name?
4 How do you ask the elderly gentleman where he's from?
5 Where are the following from, and are they men or women?
a Soy española
b Soy galesa
c Soy irlandés
d Soy francés

QUIZ

1 *Time for a break* See if you can write these sentences out with the correct gaps between the words (punctuation too, if you're feeling brave):

a **comotellamas**
b **mellamoisabelytu**
c **esustedinglesanosoyescocesa**

2 *Anagram* Sort these anagrams out to make words you know:

a **sdeut** b **amlol** c **¿móoc?**

3 *Stopgap* Fill in the missing letters in these phrases (one letter per dot):

a **¿Cómo te ll.. as?**
b **¿Es us.. d español?**
c **Sí, s.. de Madrid.**

Spanish Surnames

Most Spaniards have two surnames, their mother's as well as their father's (which comes first).

So a visitor who writes his name as John Peter Brown could find himself being called Señor Peter.

Spaniards use both surnames for everything
- Visiting card
- Bank accounts
- All official documents

When introducing people in Spain you tend to use their first surnames.

Origins

A Spaniard is **un español** or **una española.** But people also have a word for their regional origin.

Region	Name
Andalucía	andaluz/andaluza
Galicia	gallego/gallega
Cataluña	catalán/catalana

Likewise, for the city, town or village of origin

City	Name
Madrid	**madrileño/madrileña**
Valencia	**valenciano/valenciana**
Málaga	**malagueño/malagueña**

Pamplona, in Navarra, on the edge of the Basque country, has one of the most famous festivals in Spain – la fiesta de San Fermín

WHAT LANGUAGE DO YOU SPEAK?

RACIÓN 4

WHEN IN SPAIN ...
The language we call Spanish (**español**) is, strictly speaking, Castilian (**castellano**) so you'll hear it referred to by both names. And it's very useful to be able to ask which languages people speak.

- To ask 'Do you speak English?'
¿Habla usted inglés?

- To say 'I speak . . .'
Hablo $\begin{cases} \textbf{inglés} \\ \textbf{español} \end{cases}$

- 'I don't speak'
No hablo

Galícià, Cabanas – repairing nets

ACTION

Andrew and Laura are walking down the Ramblas in Barcelona. They come to the bird market and Andrew persuades Laura to talk to a parrot.

Laura **¿Habla usted inglés?**
(no reply)
Laura *(a bit disappointed)* **¿Habla usted español?**
(Still no reply; and the parrot hangs upside down.)

Miguel asks a policeman if he speaks languages; not surprisingly, he speaks a bit of French – but the Arabic is rather unusual!

Miguel **¿Habla usted idiomas?**
Policía **Pues, hablo un poquito el francés, y el árabe.**
Miguel **Gracias. Y el español, claro.**
Policía **Sí, por supuesto.**

Miguel asks Juan Pérez, who's from Valencia, what languages he speaks.

Miguel **¿Hablas idiomas?**
Juan **Sí, hablo inglés y francés.**
Miguel **Pero, ¿hablas valenciano?**
Juan **Hablo valenciano.**

REPLAY

1 When you ask somebody if he/she speaks English, you have two choices: **¿Habla usted inglés?** (rather formal) or: **¿Hablas inglés?** (more friendly).

2 The word for languages is **idiomas**, as in: **¿Habla usted idiomas?** The names of languages are the same as the *masculine* words for nationalities: **inglés, francés, galés** etc.

3 If you think **Hablo español** is a bit of an exaggeration, be honest like the policeman and say: **un poco** or **un poquito** (a little bit).

4 **Claro** and **por supuesto** mean just about the same: use them if someone says something obvious and you want to reply 'Of course'.

5 People very often start a sentence with **Pues**... It simply means 'Well ...'

TRYOUT

1 You go to change some money at the bank. Ask the clerk if she speaks English. (Use the word **usted** for 'you').

2 The person you are sitting next to at a bar smiles and asks you: **¿Habla usted español?** What would you reply? (Be realistic!)

3 You've spoken a few words in Spanish to the lady staying at the next villa, but now you need a bit of English. How would you ask her if she speaks English? (Use **tú** for 'you').

4 Read Ración 3 before doing this. How would you say:
a I speak English but I'm Scottish. ('but' is *pero*)
b I'm English and I speak Spanish a bit.
c I'm Welsh and I speak English and Welsh.

Don't forget: men and women will give slightly different answers.

QUIZ

1 *Wrongwrite* Three of the words in this list actually exist, the others don't. Give yourself 30 seconds to pick out and write down those which *do* exist (forget the rest!):

hablat, hablo habler, hablu, hablas, habli, hablos, hablet, habla, hablur.

2 *Jumblies* The words in these two sentences have been jumbled up. Try to sort them out and write them down: check you know what they mean. Time allowed – 60 seconds.

a **¿inglés usted habla?**
b **poco español el hablo un**

3 *On the way to Santiago* **Santiago de Compostela** was (and is) a place of international pilgrimage. The question here is: Can you make up from its letters the four main nationalities of the UK, using letters as often as you like?

4 Which languages are spoken in these countries

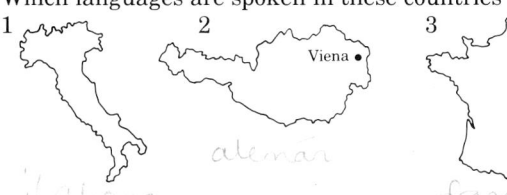

Spain's languages
Many Spaniards speak another local language as well as Castilian Spanish.

In the tourist belt along the East coast and especially in the area around Barcelona, many people speak Catalan (**catalán**) – a language between Spanish and French. Slightly further South they speak Valencian (**valenciano**), very closely related to Catalan.

In the North West part of Spain (Galicia) just north of Portugal, they speak **gallego** – a language between Portuguese and Spanish.

In the Basque country, an area close to the French border, they speak Basque (**vasco**) a language old, mysterious and unlike any other.

In Franco's day these regional languages were frowned upon, even outlawed, but regional languages are very popular today. Often public signs are printed in Castilian *and* the regional language – if not, the locals sometimes come along and spray their language on.

Galícià – cathedral of Santiago de Copostela

FINDING YOUR WAY AROUND

RACIÓN 5

WHEN IN SPAIN ...
Most Spaniards are eager to help visitors find their way around; so eager, they'll sometimes accompany you all the way. One thing is remembering how to ask the way, but another is understanding the reply. You'll be set on the right track with a wave of the arm so you could keep asking and reach your destination in a series of single hops.

- To ask your way, name the place and say 'please'!
La oficina de Turismo, (Tourist office) ⎫
Correos, (Post Office) ⎬ **por favor**

- You can begin with 'where is . . .?' if you want:
¿Dónde está Correos? (Post Office)

- To ask 'where are . . .?'
¿Dónde están los servicios (toilets)

- There are three vital directions:
left	**a la izquierda**
right	**a la derecha**
straight on	**todo recto** / todo derecho

Madrid – station signs

ACTION

Andrew asks his way to the post office.

Andrew ¿Correos, por favor?
Woman ¿Correos? Es la primera calle a la derecha y la segunda a la izquierda.
Andrew **Muchas gracias.**
Woman **De nada.**

Miguel is looking for the Tourist Office

Miguel **¿Dónde está la Oficina de Turismo, por favor?**
Señora **¿La Oficina de Turismo? Está por allí, a la izquierda.**

Miguel asks a young lady where the taxi rank is. He has to go straight on, and it's in the town centre.

Miguel **Por favor, señorita, ¿dónde está la parada de taxis?**
Girl **Allí, todo recto, en el centro de la ciudad.**
Miguel **Gracias.**
Girl **De nada.**

In a café, Miguel needs a toilet.

Miguel **¡Oiga por favor! ¿Dónde están los servicios?**
Barman **Al fondo, a la izquierda.**
Miguel **Gracias.**

REPLAY

1 The simplest formula for asking the way is: **¿Correos, por favor?** (The post office please?) A bit more precise is: **¿Dónde está la Oficina de Turismo, por favor? Oiga** means 'listen', but it's a perfectly normal way of saying 'excuse me'.

2 Apart from **izquierda, derecha** and **todo recto**, one or two other replies might be: **aquí** (here), **allí** (there), **por allí** (that way); **en el centro de la ciudad** (in the town centre); toilets in cafes always seem to be **al fondo** (at the back).

3 'First' is **primera** and 'second' is **segunda** referring to streets.

4 The word **Correos** (post office) behaves in a funny way: word for word, it means 'mails', but it's used to mean 'Post Office' – and doesn't need a word for 'the'.

TRYOUT

1 You're looking for the Tourist Office in a new town, so you do the obvious – ask a policeman! You're a bit nervous, so use the simplest phrase possible.

2 You're staying at the Hotel Esmeralda, but have got a bit lost after visiting the port. You see a friendly face approaching. What do you ask?

3 You want to buy a stamp or two, and know the post office isn't far away. How do you ask the way there? Use either the short or the longer question.

4 The reply you hear is: **Está en el centro. Por allí, todo recto, y a la izquierda.** Which way do you go?

QUIZ

1 *Missing letter* In this list are all the letters you need to make up the three directions you should now understand in Spanish. All, that is, except one. Which one?

   a c d e h i l o q r t z

2 *Mini-orienteering* On holiday in Benidorm, George is trying to identify a few places, so he bravely asks a policeman. The conversation has become a bit jumbled – Can you sort out the questions and replies?

a **Buenos días**
b **¿La Oficina de Turismo, por favor?**
c **¿Correos, por favor?**
d **¿El Bar Manolo, por favor?**

i **Allí, a la izquierda**
ii **Allí, a la derecha**
iii **Buenos días**
iv **Todo recto**

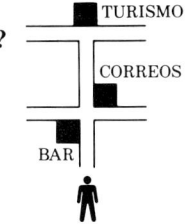

Public conveniences

Gents is **Caballeros**
Ladies is **Señoras**

But mostly there are good clear symbols on the doors. And the general word for lavatories is **Servicios.**

If you really only want to wash your hands look for **Lavabos** or **Aseos**. (But, both of these are also often another way of saying loos/lavatories/toilets.)

Street names
You'll find the same words recurring over and over again.
Calle is simply 'street' as in *Calle de la Virgen del Socorro* (in Tossa)
Plaza is 'square' as in *Plaza Real* (in Barcelona)
Avenida is a broad, usually tree-lined, avenue as in *Avenida de América* (in Madrid)
Paseo is tree-lined with a broad walkway where people can enjoy an evening 'paseo'* or walkabout – as in *Paseo de Recoletos* (in Madrid)

Carretera

*The 'paseo' is the ritual evening walk – usually up and down a particular street in any town.

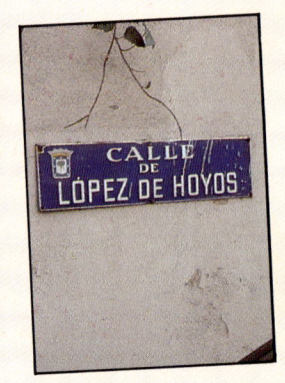

TRYING THE TAPAS

RACIÓN 6

WHEN IN SPAIN...
Standing around drinking without nibbling something is fairly uncommon in Spain. So most bars and cafés offer snacks, usually prepared on the premises. The most typical of these are **tapas**.

• To ask what **tapas** they have, say:
¿Qué tapas tienen?
The answer will be 'We have...'
Tenemos...

• Another way is to ask 'Are there any..?'
¿Hay { **calamares?** (squids)
          gambas? (prawns)

Tapas

ACTION

Andrew has heard about **tapas,** so he goes into the Bar Don Juan to see if they have any squid.

Andrew **¿Hay calamares?**
Barman **No hay calamares. Pero tenemos jamón serrano.**
Andrew **Muy bien.**
Barman (dishing it up)
 Una porción de jamón serrano.

Miguel asks what **tapas** are available, and orders two portions – one of prawns, one of cuttlefish.

Miguel **Hola, buenas tardes. ¿Qué tapas tienen?**
Waiter **Pues tenemos sepia a la plancha, calamares a la romana, mejillones, gambas, tortilla española ...**
Miguel **Pues una de gambas a la plancha y otra de sepia. ¡Ah! Y una cerveza, por favor.**
Waiter **Vale.**

REPLAY

1 **Hay** is a very valuable word: it means 'there is...' and 'there are...' **Hay gambas** (There are prawns). As a question it means 'Is there any..?' or 'Are there any..?' **¿Hay vino blanco?** (Is there any white wine?) **¿Hay gambas?** (Are there any prawns?)

2 **¿Qué?** (a favourite word of Manuel's) means 'what?' So **¿Qué tapas hay?** (What tapas are there?) and **¿Qué tapas tienen?** (What tapas have you got?)

3 Spaniards miss things out just like English-speakers. So Miguel's **Una (ración) de gambas a la plancha y otra (ración) de sepia** should make sense as 'One (portion) of grilled prawns and another (portion) of cuttlefish.'

4 There are various ways of saying 'Have you got...?' and they all start **¿Tien...**
¿Tiene.... (to one person-formal)
¿Tienes... (to one person you're friendly with)
¿Tienen... (to the shop in general)

5 When you place an order the waiter or waitress will often say **vale**. It means 'OK' or 'Fine'.

TRYOUT

1 A bit peckish, you go into a bar one evening with a friend who thinks they sell **tapas** there. The barman comes over; what do you say?

2 The barman says: **Pues tenemos tortilla española, sepia, gambas, mejillones...** You'd like a portion of prawns and one of omelette, if possible. Order them if you think they're available.

3 Don't forget the drinks. Your friend would like a glass of red wine, you'd like a beer.

QUIZ

1 *Breaker* This dialogue has been written without any spaces. Try to write it out as separate words, with a new line for each change of person speaking. Extra credit for correct punctuation!

Buenastardeshaytapassihaygambastortillaycal amaresdosracionesdetortillayunadegambaspor favor

2 *Matchmaker* Match each question or each request with its appropriate reply:

a **¿Hay tapas?**
b **Una ración de gambas, por favor.**
c **Dos raciones de tortilla,**
d **¿Qué tapas tienen?**

i **Vale.**
ii **Tenemos tortilla, aceitunas y sepia.**
iii **No tenemos gambas.**
iv **Sí, hay sepia y mejillones.**

The best tapas

Originally when you ordered a sherry in Spain they covered the top of your glass with a tiny saucer, on which was placed a tit-bit. The word for 'to cover' up is **tapar** – hence **tapas**. Today you're still sometimes given a small plate of olives, nuts or crisps. Or you can pay and get **una ración,** or **una porción,** quite a big portion. They can be so delicious that you can find yourself making a whole meal of them. Overleaf are some favourites.

Favourite Tapas

Calamares – squid
Tortilla española – Spanish (potato) omelette
Caracoles – snails
Patatas alioli – cold boiled potatoes with garlic mayonnaise
Patatas a la brava – hot fried potatoes with spicy tomato sauce
Queso manchego – cheese from La Mancha
Champiñones – mushrooms
Aceitunas – olives
Pinchos morunos – small pieces of pork, kebab style
Mejillones – mussels
Empanadillas – fish or meat pasty
Gambas – prawns (can be enormous)
Pulpo – octopus
Sepia – cuttlefish
Jamón serrano – naturally cured ham
Ensaladilla rusa – Russian salad
Anything... **a la plancha** is grilled
     ... **a la romana** is deep-fried in batter.

Some of these are regional specialities; you will find that they are not all available everywhere in Spain.

SHOPPING FOR FOOD AND DRINK

RACIÓN 7

WHEN IN SPAIN...
If you're touring, or self-catering, or fancy a picnic, it can be quite an experience to shop at the grocer's or in a fruit and vegetable market.

- You name what you want, with a quantity:
Medio kilo de cerezas (half a kilo of cherries).

A longer phrase: **¿Me da usted..?** (Can I have...?).

- Usually the assistant will say 'Anything else?'
¿Algo más?

To which you say
No gracias, or **Sí,** and go on to the next thing.

- If you can't see what you want, ask 'Have you got..?
¿Tiene vino de barril? (wine from the barrel)

Palma de Mallorca – indoor market

ACTION

Miguel buys half a kilo of cherries in the market.

Miguel	¿Me da usted, por favor, medio kilo de cerezas?
Woman	Sí, en seguida... Aquí tiene... ¿Algo más?
Miguel	No, gracias. ¿Cuánto es?
Woman	Doscientas treinta.
Miguel	Un momento. Doscientas treinta. Muchas gracias.
Woman	No hay de qué.

Andrew buys some items for a picnic.

Andrew	Buenas tardes.
Assistant	Buenas tardes.
Andrew	Quiero comprar un poco por un pic...
Assistant	Merienda.
Andrew	Sí. Merienda. Un poco de queso, típico de...
Assistant	¿Del país, de la región?
Andrew	De la región, sí. Aragón. Cien gramos.
Assistant	Sí, sí
Andrew	¿Y jamón?
Assistant	¿Jamón serrano de Teruel?
Andrew	Sí, jamón serrano. Tres lonjas por favor. (pointing to a dish) ¿Qué es esto?
Assistant	Tortilla de patatas.
Andrew	Ah sí, muy bien, una tortilla por favor.

Carmen is in a wine cellar to buy rosé wine from the barrel.

Carmen	Hola.
Girl	Hola, dime.
Carmen	¿Tienes vino rosado de barril?
Girl	Sí
Carmen	Un litro.
Girl	Vale. (She goes to the barrel) Un litro de rosado, ¿no?
Carmen	Sí (She draws off the wine)
Girl	¿Algo más?
Carmen	No, gracias. ¿Cuánto es?
Girl	Noventa y siete pesetas.

REPLAY

1 Time to check your weights: **un kilo** (1kg); **medio kilo** (½kg); **doscientos gramos** (200g); **cien gramos** (100g). The nearest equivalent to a ¼lb is **cien gramos;** the nearest thing to 1lb is **medio kilo**. Less precisely, you can ask for **un poco de ...** (a little). Liquids are sold by the **litro** (1¾ pints).

2 There are some set phrases useful for shopping. You can say: **¿Cuánto es?** (How much is it?) **Nada más, gracias** (Nothing else thanks.) And you will hear: **Aquí tiene.** (Here you are); and of course the numbers – they're listed on p.82.

TRYOUT

1 You aim to have a picnic on your way to the next town, so you go to a small food shop. Say 'Hello' and ask for a little cheese.

2 You see some of that nice naturally-cured ham, so you ask for 200 grams.

3 The man behind the counter asks: **¿Algo más?** You think that's all you'll get here, so what do you say?

4 Ask him how much it comes to.

5 He says: **Trescientas ochenta pesetas.** How much do you give him?

QUIZ

1 *Sliced food* Some common foods and drinks have been cut up, and their syllables rearranged. Can you sort them out and write out the five correctly? If you're feeling confident, try putting in the accents (not shown here):

   quemon, chochichon, jano, viso, salrizo.

2 *Codewords* Some common shopping phrases have been disguised by moving all their letters one place along in the alphabet. What are they?

a **brvj ujfof**
b **¿nf eb ...?**
c **¿bmhp nbt?**
d **obeb nbt**
e **¿dvboup ft?**

3 *Weightwatching* Match the phrase with the figure.

a **Doscientos cincuenta gramos**   (i) **½kg**
b **Cien gramos**   (ii) **250g**
c **Medio kilo**   (iii) **1kg**
d **Un cuarto de kilo**   (iv) **¼kg**
e **Un kilo**   (v) **100g**

Shopping

The 'corner grocer's' still exists in Spain – **ultramarinos, comestibles** or **alimentación.** But as elsewhere the general trend is towards self-service supermarkets **(supermercados),** and near big cities **hipermercados** (hypermarkets). And of course there's the ordinary **mercado** or market. Most cities have excellent covered markets and most towns have a regular market day. In markets the service is almost always boisterous and chatty.

On price tags and signs you will sometimes see some abbreviations: **ptas**=pesetas, **p.v.p.**=precio de venta al público (retail price).

Not all shops sell the same things as their British equivalents – for example, a **droguería** sells paints, brushes and cleaning materials, the **farmacia** (chemist's) sells only medicine and health products.

Watch out for **pastelerías** (cake shops) which are often attached to **panaderías** – the state-run bread shops. Spanish cakes and sweets can be excellent – particularly **turrón** – made of almonds and honey – and **mazapán,** like you've never tasted.

tienda

Street market

SHOPPING FOR GIFTS

RACIÓN 8

WHEN IN SPAIN
Spain is generally considered good value when it comes to buying gifts and souvenirs and most places offer a range of local and national craftsmanship, like pottery, leather goods, Toledan steel, carved wooden figures etc. The price may be marked, but it may not... so you'll have to be ready to ask.

- To ask 'How much is...?

¿Cuánto vale { **el bikini verde?** (the green bikini)
{ **esta bota de vino?** (this wine skin)

- If you want to buy it, say:

Muy bien or **bueno**

If not, just say 'thanks' and move on:

gracias.

ACTION

Carmen asks the price of a green bikini.

Carmen	**Hola, buenas tardes.**
Girl	**Buenas tardes.**
Carmen	**¿Cuánto vale el bikini verde?**
Girl	**Cinco mil pesetas.**
Carmen	**Vale, gracias.**
Girl	**De nada, hasta luego.**

Carmen asks about a leather wine-skin, but doesn't buy it.

Carmen	**Perdone. ¿Cuánto vale esta bota de vino?**
Girl	**Un momento. Mil seiscientas pesetas.**
Carmen	**Gracias.**
Girl	**De nada.**

Miguel asks the price of some shoes and something else that he just points to.

Miguel	**Oiga, señorita, por favor. ¿Cuánto valen estos zapatos?**
Girl	**Dos mil doscientas cincuenta pesetas.**
Miguel	**¿Cuanto vale esto?**
Girl	**Quinientas pesetas.**
Miguel	**Gracias.**
Girl	**A usted.**

REPLAY

1 To ask the price of something, say: **¿Cuánto vale..?** (How much is..?) or **¿Cuánto valen..?** (How much are..?) Then wait for the torrent of numbers! (Time for more practice – see page 82.) If you don't catch the price first time, say **¿Cómo?** (what?)

2 There are two words for 'this' (**este, esta**) and two for 'these' (**estos, estas**). Sex rears its head again; the first of each pair is used for masculine words, the second for feminine. Check the details on page 75. note 2. **Esto** means 'this' when you point to something without naming it.

3 Spanish puts the word for colours *after* the name of the thing. So 'the green bikini' is **el bikini verde,** 'the white shirt' is **la camisa blanca,** and 'white wine' is **vino blanco.** (For more information see page 75.)

4 For a longer list of clothes in Spanish, see page 83.

TRYOUT

1 In a clothes shop, you see a shirt that you like. Ask how much it costs.

2 The lady says: **Cuatro mil cuatrocientas cincuenta pesetas.** You aim to spend no more than five thousand pesetas – can you buy it?

3 Congratulations. Say 'That's OK'.

4 Then you see some very attractive shoes. Ask how much they cost.

5 The lady says: **Seiscientas treinta y cinco.** How much are they?

6 Thank her and walk away.

7 In a gift shop you see a Toledo steel paper-knife but you don't know the word for it. How would you ask the price?

QUIZ

1 *Weak endings* The endings to these phrases have been separated from the beginnings. Can you sort them out?

a ¿Cuánto vale este...
b Estos zapatos...
c ¿Cuánto vale...
d Setecientas...
e ¿Cuánto valen...

i valen seis mil veinte pesetas
ii estas camisas?
iii pesetas
iv bikini rojo?
v esta bota de vino?

2 *A-mazing* Start with the 'c', then move in any direction, one letter at a time, to find a question very useful when you're out shopping. To be really clever, put in accents and punctuation too...

```
S T A S
E C U A
N A V N
E L O T
```

You may want to buy a porrón as a souvenir, but lengthy and enjoyable practice is needed to master the art

GETTING HOTEL ACCOMMODATION

RACIÓN 9

WHEN IN SPAIN...
If you're moving around Spain you'll need to be able to find accommodation. Look out for the words **hotel** (hotel), **pensión** (boarding house), **residencia** (hotel without meals) or simply **camas** (beds) by the roadside.

- To ask 'Have you got a room free?':
¿Tiene una habitación libre?

- They will ask you a series of questions:
¿Para cuántas noches? (for how many nights?)
¿Para cuántas personas? (for how many people?)
¿Con baño? (with bath?)

Residencia

ACTION
At a hotel, Andrew explains he has a reservation.

Receptionist	**Buenos días**
Andrew	**Buenos días. Me llamo Andrew Sachs, y tengo una reservación.**
Receptionist	**Muy bien, señor Sachs. El pasaporte, por favor.**
Andrew	**Sí. Pasaporte**
Receptionist	**Es la habitación número trescientos veintiuno.**

Miguel hasn't booked ahead, but he manages to get a double room with bathroom for two nights.

Miguel	**Buenas noches**
Receptionist	**(Sí), buenas noches**
Miguel	**¿Tiene una habitación libre?**
Receptionist	**Sí. ¿Para esta noche?**
Miguel	**Para esta noche y para mañana. Para hoy y mañana.**
Receptionist	**Sí. ¿Para cuántas personas?**
Miguel	**Para dos personas.**
Receptionist	**Sí, tenemos. ¿Con baño o con ducha?**
Miguel	**Con baño, por favor.**
Receptionist	**Sí, de acuerdo.**

REPLAY

1 The different sorts of room you can get are:
una habitación doble – a double room
una habitación individual – a single room
You'll see the word for 'double' and 'single' goes after 'room' in Spanish. For a bit more on this see page 75, note 2.

2 Your room can be **con baño** (with a bathroom) or **con ducha** (with a shower). Or, if you're not too bothered, **sin baño** (without a bathroom).

3 If you have reserved, just say: **Tengo una reservación** (or **reserva**).

4 **Para** ('for') is a useful word in hotels: **¿Para cuántas noches?** (For how many nights?); **¿Para cuántas personas?** (For how many people?) To reply, just slot in the number: **para dos personas, para una noche** (For two people, for one night); **para hoy** (for today); **para mañana** (for tomorrow).

TRYOUT

1 You and your spouse arrive dusty and weary at a roadside hotel. Ask the receptionist if he has a double room.

2 The receptionist says yes and asks: **¿Con baño o con ducha?** A shower is fine by you. What do you say?

3 Then he asks **¿Para cuántas noches?** You'd like to stay two nights, so what do you say?

4 The receptionist says: **El pasaporte, por favor?** What do you do?

5 You are given the key with the information **La habitación número ciento treinta y ocho.** You *could* look at the number, but you think you've understood. Have you? Where do you head for?

QUIZ

1 *Wordsnake* Follow the snake from left to right to find the number of your room. Where words overlap, the common letter is not repeated. Add accents where necessary, if you can:

lahabitacionumerochocientosiete

2 *About your room* The words in the crossword are all connected with information about your hotel room:

1 Número 900 **2 Con... o ducha** **3 ¿... o doble?**
4 No tiene baño completo, pero sí tiene...

N	O	V	E	C	I	E	N	T	O	S
B	A	Ñ	O							
I	N	D	I	V	I	D	U	A	L	
D	U	C	H	A						

Camp sites

There are more than 500 camp sites in Spain. Many have excellent shops and restaurants and are well organised.

It's sensible to book at coastal sites during the holiday months and camping carnets are worth bringing.

Hotels – What the stars mean
In Spain hotels are starred on a scale of from 1 to 5, and are cheaper than in the United Kingdom. Anything with four or five stars is generally in the luxury class. A three star hotel will usually give you your own separate bathroom and room service. Even one-star hotels can be very comfortable – but it's best to check.

Your own eyes and instinct are usually the best guides in choosing accommodation, especially as it is found under a confusing number of names like:

hostal – economic hotel
residencia – ditto
pensión – simple hotel with some long-term residents
casa de húespedes – boarding house
camas – just 'beds'
habitaciones – rooms

Paradores – These are very luxurious state-run hotels often sited out of town in beauty spots (though the parador in Granada is actually inside the Moorish palace, La Alhambra). They're pricey, but very good value.

PAUSE FOR A SNACK

RACIÓN 10

WHEN IN SPAIN...
If you're feeling peckish you can get a sandwich (**un bocadillo**) in most bars and cafés. Another popular snack in Spain is **churros** (deep-fried, crispy, doughnut batter). If you need cooling down, an ice cream (**un helado**) might be the answer.

- To ask 'What sandwiches have you got?':
¿Qué bocadillos tiene? (or ... **tienes?**)
They'll tell you a list, and you choose like this:
Uno de queso, por favor. (A cheese one, please.)

- The same applies to ice creams:
¿Qué helados tiene?
Uno de chocolate, por favor.

- If you like, you can start your order with 'Can I have ...?'
¿Me da { **un helado de vainilla?** (a vanilla ice cream)
{ **un bocadillo de jamón?** (a ham sandwich)

Tossa de Mar – Andrew tries the helados

ACTION

Miguel's niece, Beatriz, asks what sandwiches are available, and decides to have an omelette sandwich.

Beatriz	**Buenos días. ¿Qué bocadillos tiene?**
Barman	**Jamón, queso, tortilla, calamar, sepia, chorizo ...**
Beatriz	**Uno de tortilla, por favor.**

cuttlefish

In Tossa Andrew fancies an ice cream. He points to the one he wants on the display.

Andrew	**Uno de éstos, por favor.**
Lady	**Muy bien.**

Carmen has a lot of ice-cream flavours to choose from, but finally goes for the pistacho.

Carmen	**¡Hola! ¿Qué helados tienes?**
Girl	**Pues, mira: tengo vainilla, chocolate, fresa, limón, turrón, pistacho, estrachatela ... Dime, ¿cuál quieres?**
Carmen	**Uno de pistacho, por favor.**
Girl	(suggests a cone) **¿Así ...?**
Carmen	**Sí**
Girl	**Allí tienes.**
Carmen	**Muchas gracias.**
Girl	**Son noventa pesetas.**
Carmen	**Vale.**

stracciatela

Miguel wants a milkshake.

Miguel	**Oiga, por favor. ¿Qué batidos tiene?**
Waitor	**Tenemos chocolate, fresa, nata, vainilla, turrón ...**
Miguel	**Uno de fresa por favor.**

Miguel is a bit peckish, so he buys 50 pesetas-worth of **churros**.

Miguel	**Buenos días, señora.**
Lady	**Buenos días. Dígame, dígame.**
Miguel	**¿Me da una de churros, por favor?**
Lady	**Sí, señor ... ¿Cuántos quiere? Eh, ¿cincuenta pesetas?**
Miguel	**Sí, cincuenta.**
Lady	**Vale ... Allí tiene usted.**

REPLAY

1 A ham sandwich is **un bocadillo de jamón**, a cheese sandwich **un bocadillo de queso**. For more types of sandwich, see page 78, note 2. Notice the word order in Spanish: 'a sandwich of ham'. Other examples are **un zumo de naranja** (an orange juice) and **un helado de chocolate** (a chocolate ice cream).

2 **uno** and **una** both mean 'one' as well as 'a'. So **uno de pistacho** means 'a pistachio one' and **una (ración) de churros** means 'one (portion) of churros'.

3 People will talk back at you! Here are a few more phrases you may need to recognise: **¿Para beber?** (Would you like to order a drink?); **¿Cuál quiere(s)?** (Which one would you like?); **¿Cuántos quiere?** (How many would you like?); **¿Así?** (Like this?); **Dime** (Can I help you?); **En seguida** (Right away); **Allí tiene.** (There you are); **Tome.** (Here you are); **De acuerdo** (OK).

TRYOUT

1 One evening you go into a bar with a friend, and ask what sandwiches they have. What do you say?
2 There doesn't seem to be much choice: cheese and omelette. Order one of each.
3 To drink, you'd like an orange juice and a beer.
4 Now order two ice-creams: a pistachio and a vanilla.
5 On the way back, your friend is still peckish, so he talks you into buying him about 50 pesetas-worth of **churros** at the **churrería**. What do you say?

QUIZ

1 *Scrambled order* These orders for something to eat have got mixed up. Can you unscramble them?

    tortilla de un favor por bocadillo

    ¿pesetas me de da cincuenta churros?

2 *Sore thumb* In each of these groups of words, one sticks out like a sore thumb. Try to find it

a **Jamón, bocadillo, chorizo, queso**
b **Vainilla, almendra, chocolate, churro**
c **Zumo, tapa, bocadillo, helado**

Sandwiches

Bocadillos are sandwiches – usually of French-style bread – filled with cheese (*queso*), omelette (*tortilla*), spiced sausage (*chorizo, salchichón, longaniza* – the choice is wide!). The bread is usually not buttered, but sometimes (especially in Catalonia) it is rubbed with tomato and/or a little garlic to give it extra flavour. *Un sandwich* is usually a toasted sandwich made with sliced bread, with a filling of cheese and/or ham. A relative newcomer is the *sandwich vegetal*, with its filling of salad and mayonnaise.

Other snacks

A typical Spanish snack to have between meals, or at breakfast, is *churros* – a deep-fried batter sprinkled with sugar and sold in a rolled-up paper cone. They can be eaten with hot chocolate in the evening at a café, or even bought at a stall, and eaten from a packet in the street. Look for the sign *Churrería*.

Not only are ice creams (*helados*) doubly welcome in the heat of the summer, they also come in a wide range of flavours. Some of the less usual ones are *almendra* (almond), *turrón* (nougat) and a *vainilla* (vanilla) which actually tastes of vanilla. Also try an interesting sweet drink – *horchata*, which looks like milk but but is made from tiger nuts.

BEING SOCIABLE

RACIÓN 11

WHEN IN SPAIN ...
When you start talking to Spaniards, as to anyone else, a subject that soon arises is family and jobs.

- To say you're single:

Soy { **soltero** (man)
      soltera (woman)

or married:

Estoy { **casado** (man)
        casada (woman)

- To say 'I've got children, brothers, sisters ...' etc:

Tengo { **dos niños** (two children)   niñas
        un hermano (one brother)   hermana

ACTION
Miguel talked to a man called Francisco Pardo from a town called Alzira.

Miguel	**¿Cómo se llama usted?**
FP	**Me llamo Francisco Pardo.**
Miguel	**¿De dónde es usted?**
FP	**Soy de Alzira.**
Miguel	**¿En qué trabaja usted?**
FP	**Soy profesor.**
Miguel	**¿Está usted casado?**
FP	**No, soy soltero.**

Then he spoke to a schoolboy called Bernardo.

Miguel	**¿Cómo te llamas?**
Bernardo	**Me llamo Bernardo.**
Miguel	**¿Tienes hermanos?**
Bernardo	**No. ¡Hermanas!**
Miguel	**¿Cuántas hermanas tienes?**
Bernardo	**Una.**
Miguel	**Una. Y ¿cómo se llama?**
Bernardo	**Sara.**

REPLAY

1 Have a look at Ración 3. It will tell you how to say where you come from and what your name is.

2 Notice that when you are asking a person questions about herself – or himself, you have to decide between the two words for you: **usted** and **tú**. Depending on which you use, the endings of verbs will vary a little. For more on this, see note 5, page 76.

3 To ask someone what job they do, say: **¿En qué trabaja(s)?** (In what do you work?). The answer is **Soy ...** with the word for your job. You don't say the word for 'a':

Soy profesor(a) (I'm a teacher). **Soy ama de casa** (I'm a housewife). (For a list of jobs see page 86).

4 The words for 'married' (**casado/casada**) and 'single' (**soltero/soltera**) both have alternative endings: 'a' for women, 'o' for men. More on page 75, note 2. They also use a different word for 'I am'. **Estoy casada. Soy soltera.**

5 If you want to ask somebody the same question they've just asked you, use: **¿Y tú?** or **¿Y usted?**

TRYOUT

1 You strike up a conversation with a lady you've seen before in your hotel. She asks you: **¿Cómo te llamas?** What do you reply?

2 She asks you where you're from. What do you reply?

3 Bounce the question back to her.

4 She says: **Soy sevillana.** Where do you think she is from?

5 Your Spanish feels pretty good by now, so you decide to ask a question yourself. Ask her what her job is. (Use the word **tú** for 'you').

6 She replies: **Soy representante de una empresa de plásticos.** What have you gathered from that?

QUIZ

1 *National disaster* These nationalities have got mixed up. Can you sort them out? Some refer to males, some to females, so watch the endings. And don't forget to put in accents where necessary.

a **aloñsepa**   b **essocaec**   c **saderlin**
d **lesag**   e **glinse**

2 *Identity crisis* These questions and answers have somehow melted together. Can you separate them and write them out as three questions, each one with a reply? Don't forget the punctuation!

comotellamas	**dedondeeres**
soydeyork	**soysecretaria**
enquetrabajas	**mellamoclara**

3 *Jobhunting* Four jobs from the list on page 86 have been sliced up into syllables and spread around. Try to put them together again. Some refer to men, some to women.

sec de re ta a ple do em pro pen dien ria fe ra so te

secretaria profesora empleado dependiente

Spain – Fascinating Facts
The Country
• Spain is higher than any other European country–except Switzerland. Much of its interior is over 2500 feet and this often accounts for the beautifully clear light. Spain is a country of artists and for artists.
• From 1961 to '73 there was an 'economic miracle'; Spain is now the world's 9th industrial power.
• There is a very sharp contrast between the rich and poor areas of Spain. The countryside has lost much of its population to the cities over the last twenty years. Average earnings in the most depopulated and poorest areas – Andalusia, Estremadura and Galicia – are less than half of those in the richest areas – Madrid, Barcelona and the Basque region.

Tourism
• Tourism – the number of tourists who come to Spain each year is larger than the total population.
• In 1959 just three million tourists visited Spain, by 1973 the total had risen to thirty-four million and is now over forty million.
• The Portuguese and the French go to Spain more often than anyone else, but about six million British people – and another five million from Germany – take Spanish holidays each year.

Castile – windmills like these tempted Don Quixote

Tossa de Mar – high season in one of the Costa Brava's prettiest resorts

CAR WISE

RACIÓN 12

WHEN IN SPAIN ...
Petrol stations (**gasolineras** or **estaciones de servicio**) can be few and far between on the open road, and you'll find that self-service is not widespread. So you may have to use Spanish.

credit cards — tarjetas de crédito

- There are three ways of buying petrol:
by price
dos mil pesetas de súper, por favor;
by quantity
treinta litros de súper, por favor;
or by buying a full tank
lleno de súper, por favor.

el depósito lleno

Huelva – petrol station

sin plomo
gas oil / diesel / gasóleo

ACTION

Andrew orders 30 litres of 4-star, changes his mind to a full tank, and just manages to understand the price. The attendant wishes him a safe journey.

Andrew	**Buenos días.**
Attendant	**Buenos días.**
Andrew	**Treinta litros, por favor.**
Attendant	**Muy bien.**
Andrew	**No, no, lleno, lleno...Muchas gracias. ¿Cuánto es?**
Attendant	**Dos mil doscientas ochenta.**
Andrew	**Otra vez, por favor**
Attendant	**Dos mil doscientas ochenta**
Andrew	**Ah, sí...gracias**
Attendant	**¡Buen viaje!**
Andrew	**Gracias, adiós.**

Inspired by his success with the petrol, Andrew asks where the toilets are

Andrew	**¿Dónde están los servicios, por favor?**
Attendant	**Están por ahí, detrás, a la izquierda.**
Andrew	**¿Cómo?**
Attendant	**Mire, ahí, detrás, a la izquierda.**
Andrew	**Ah, sí, muchas gracias.**
Attendant	**De nada. Buenas tardes.**

REPLAY

1 **De** is used in all the different ways of ordering petrol; **tres mil pesetas de normal; veinticinco litros de súper; lleno de súper.**

2 To ask where the toilets are, use: **¿Dónde están los servicios?** See **Ración 5** for some of the replies you might hear.

3 To ask if they have other things, such as maps, use: **¿Tiene ...?** 'Have you got any ...?'

4 If you're unlucky and your car is not in good order, the simplest way to explain in the garage is to point to the part that doesn't work and say: **Esto no funciona (bien).** (This isn't working (properly). A list of car parts is given on p.85.

5 Three ways of indicating that you haven't understood: **más despacio, por favor** (more slowly, please); **otra vez, por favor** (again please) and **¿cómo?** (I beg your pardon?)

TRYOUT

1 You pull in at a service station. Your car takes 4-star; the attendant asks: **¿Normal o súper?** What do you reply?

2 Ask him to fill your car up.

3 He tells you it costs: **Tres mil doscientas veinte pesetas.** How much is that?

4 You'd like to know where the toilets are. What do you ask?

5 He replies: **Allí, a la derecha.** Where do you go?

QUIZ

1 *Wrong mixture* There are four words here that could be useful in a service station, but they're mixed up. Can you sort them out?

a **ramlon**   b **preus**
c **ericsovis** d **aspam**

2 *O for a car* Fill the spaces around these letter O's to make words connected with cars and service stations:

a _ _ _ _ **o** (up to the top)
b _ _ _ _ _ _ **ó** _ (place for buying petrol)
c _ _ _ _ **o** _ (measure for petrol)
d _ _ _ _ _ _ **o** _ (provide relief)

3 *Assembly line* The syllables of these very common phrases have been stripped down and reassembled wrongly. Can you assemble them properly?

a **vor-por-fa**
b **via-buen-je**
c **¿mas-go-al?**

Carwise

1 *Memo to Motorists*

Would-be motorists in Spain should note two basic facts:

a Spain is big: as the crow flies, the distances East-West and North-South are each equivalent to about Land's End – John O'Groats.

b You'd need to actually *be* a crow to get in a straight line from A to B – Spain is mountainous, and this can make road travel slow and tricky, so allow time.

2 Motorways

Many areas are served by good motorways (*autopistas*) and main roads (*carreteras nacionales*); especially the Mediterranean coast, the French border region and the area around Madrid, which is the centre of the Spanish communication system.

Motorways are not free; you have to pay a toll (*peaje*), depending on the distance covered. Collect a ticket as you drive on, pay as you drive off. Perhaps because of the *peaje* the motorways tend to be less used than British ones.

Costa Blanca – a mountain road

3 Petrol

Petrol is still a state monopoly in Spain, so don't look for the familiar petrol company signs. Service stations (*Estaciones de servicio*) are not so frequent as in other countries, so fill up regularly!
Petrol is bought by the litre, and there are two main grades: *Normal* (2-star) and *Súper* (4-star).

4 International Driving Licence

EEC nationals don't technically need an international driving licence. The motoring organisations, however, often recommend that you carry one with you in Spain.

TRIPS AND EXCURSIONS

RACIÓN 13

WHEN IN SPAIN ...
Excursions from your holiday resort to nearby places of interest may be arranged by tour organisations. On the other hand you may want to take the bull by the horns and arrange your own trip. In which case you'll get the information you need from the **Oficina de Turismo** (Tourist office) or the **Estación** (station) – of which there are two types: **... de trenes** (train) and **... de autobuses** (bus).

- To ask 'Are there trains/buses going to ...?'

¿Hay { **trenes** / **autobuses** } **para Barcelona?**

- To ask for a ticket

Un billete / **Dos billetes** } **para Barcelona, por favor.**

- Be prepared for this question:
¿De ida (sólo)? (Single?)
¿De ida y vuelta? (Return?)

Benidorm is on the line between Alicante and Denia

ACTION

Andrew buys a ticket for himself and his friend to go up the funicular in Barcelona. A single is all they need, as they'll be walking back down.

Andrew   **Dos billetes, por favor.**
Clerk   **¿De ida y vuelta?**
Andrew   **No, de ida sólo.**
Clerk   **Son trescientas veinte pesetas.**

Carmen buys a return bus ticket to Valencia.

Carmen   **Uno para Valencia, por favor.**
Clerk   **¿Ida o ida y vuelta?**
Carmen   **Ida y vuelta.**
Clerk   **Muy bien** (issues ticket).
           Mil cuatrocientas treinta pesetas.

This time Carmen goes by train, and asks for a timetable to find out the time of the next departure.

Carmen   **¿Hay trenes para Valencia?**
Clerk   **Sí.**
Carmen   **¿Tiene un horario, por favor?**
Clerk   **Sí, ahora mismo.**
Carmen   **Entonces, ¿cuál es el próximo?**
Clerk   **El próximo, a las seis y veinte minutos.**
Carmen   **Gracias**

REPLAY

1 The word for 'ticket' is **billete;** but you sometimes leave it out just as we can in English: **uno para Madrid** (one to Madrid); **dos para Alicante** (two to Alicante)

2 Timing is vital when you're travelling. Check how to tell the time on page 83, note 10.

3 Some key phrases for the traveller: **¿cuándo?** (when?); **¿a qué hora?** (at what time?); **¿de dónde?** (where from?) and **sale** (it leaves). So **¿Cuándo sale?** (When does it leave?) **¿De dónde sale?** (Where does it leave from?)

4 Times can be found out in the time-table (**horario**). To ask which is the next train or bus, say: **¿Cuál es el próximo?**

5 A single ticket is **un billete de ida sólo** but sometimes the **sólo** is left out.

TRYOUT

1 You want to spend a day in Alicante. At the railway station you ask for two return tickets. What do you say?
2 The booking clerk says: **Mil setecientas ochenta pesetas.** How much do you give her?
3 Ask her what time the next one is.
4 You've missed the last train back to Calpe! Rush to the bus station, and ask if there are buses to Calpe ...
5 The last one is just leaving. Ask for a single ticket.

QUIZ

Vowel trouble The following words and phrases have had their vowels (a e i o u) changed. Replace all the vowels to rebuild the words.

balloto   **ode y vaolte**
ode sulu   **¿c qaó huro?**

Public transport

• Travelling on buses and trains is relatively cheap in Spain. City buses and tubes have a usually one-fare-only system and buses are pay-as-you-enter.

• Trains called *Expreso* or *Rápido* may not be too fast. And the *Correo*, the mail train, can be excruciatingly slow.

• There are high-speed inter-city trains – *Talgo*, *ELT* and *Ter* are three of them. Not surprisingly, they cost more.

• You can buy your ticket in advance at a *RENFE* (Spanish Railways) office if you're taking a reasonably long journey. There can be delays wherever you buy your ticket but a travel agent who deals in *RENFE* tickets is often the best bet.

• Not every city has a bus terminal and even in Madrid and Barcelona long distance buses leave from different points.

• When you're reading bus and train timetables remember that *diario* means 'daily', *días laborables* are Monday to Saturday and *domingos y festivos* are Sundays and holidays.

- Air travel within Spain is well organised and for some journeys it can compete with the train on price, especially the Madrid – Barcelona shuttle.
- If you're looking at timetables or indicator boards, *salidas* means 'departures', and *llegadas* are 'arrivals'.

Madrid – taxis are plentiful and cheap

Madrid – bus stop in Calle de Segovia

EATING OUT 1

RACIÓN 14

WHEN IN SPAIN ...
The good thing about eating out in Spain is that a) there are all sorts of eating places, which means you can choose anything from a quick **tapas** snack to a long drawn out full meal, and b) there is less fuss attached to serving and eating food than you find in some countries.

• To order a single set dish, say:

el plato combinado número { **tres** / **cuatro** / **cinco** }

• To order a starter and main course:
de primero, sopa de cebolla
(to start with, onion soup)
de segundo, pollo asado
(for the main course, roast chicken)

Eating al aire libre

ACTION

Here Miguel is in a **cafetería** and he wants a set dish.

Miguel **Buenas tardes.**
Waiter **Buenas tardes.**
Miguel **Un plato combinado, por favor.**
Waiter **¿Qué número desea, señor?**
Miguel **Mm ... el cinco.**
Waiter **O sea, ¿dos huevos con beicon y patatas?**
Miguel **Sí, perfecto.**
Waiter **Muchas gracias.**

Miguel is in a small family restaurant ordering the day's set meal (**el menú**). He chooses fish soup and lamb chops.

Waiter **Buenos días. ¿Qué desea?**
Miguel **Un menú, por favor.**
Waiter **Vale.**
Miguel **De primero, sopa de pescado.**
Waiter **Sopa de pescado ... muy bien.**
Miguel **Y de segundo, chuletas de cordero.**
Waiter **Vale, muy bien.**

REPLAY

1 Ordering a **plato combinado** looks quite easy – just say the number! But notice how Spanish uses the word for 'the' when English doesn't: **El plato combinado número tres.**

2 When you say how many you would like of each item, you add a little linking **de** as well. For example:
Uno del número cinco y dos del (número) tres.

3 The word **de** crops up all over the place in menus. For example, soups:
sopa de pollo (chicken soup); **sopa de pescado** (fish soup); **sopa de ajo** (garlic soup) and many, many others. Also: **chuletas de cordero** (lamb chops); **...de cerdo** (pork chops). For a fuller list of dishes, see page 80.

4 If you have to, or want to, avoid certain kinds of food, it's useful to be able to ask whether a particular dish has got something in it. Then the word is **¿Tiene ...? ¿Tiene aceite?** Does it have oil in it? **¿Tiene ajo?** Does it have garlic in it?

5 If you want some bread with your meal say: **¿Me da un poco de pan?**

TRYOUT

1 You see a café with a fine display of **tapas,** so decide to try a few out with a friend. Order a glass of white wine and a glass of red, and a portion of Spanish omelette, prawns, Russian salad and olives.

2 You notice you haven't been given any bread. How do you ask for some?

3 The next day you see a display of **Platos combinados** in a **cafetería.** You're not sure if number three has eggs in it. How do you ask the waiter?

4 It has, so you decide to have that, and your friend wants number six. How do you order them?

QUIZ

1 *Hidden delights* Somewhere in this block of letters are hidden eight **tapas,** reading vertically or horizontally, backwards or forwards. Try to find them, referring to the list on page 78, number 2, if necessary.

```
P U B L O N U T A
A T O R T I L L A
G R U M E P A R S
A C E I T U N A S
M I R P O L E S E
B R O T H P C I P
A A N C H O A S I
S T E R M S L E A
R D S A J E M L A
```

2 *Combinations* If 3 × 2 is expressed in a **cafetería** as **Dos del tres, por favor,** give the following orders as quickly as you can:

    a 4 × 1   b 3 × 3   c 1 × 2   d 2 × 1

> **Platos combinados**
> If all you want is a single dish the best thing is to go for *un plato combinado*. You'll see them listed outside ordinary *cafeterías* – usually numbered 1, 2, 3 ...: etc and with a picture. Typical *platos combinados* are: fried fish with chips and peas; bacon, eggs and chips, pork chop with two vegetables, etc.

Platos combinados

El menú del día
You can eat very cheaply in Spanish restaurants if you take the *menú del día* (the menu of the day) or the *menú turístico*. You can get good local dishes on it, but usually the menu follows a pattern – a starter, a meat or fish dish and a simple sweet, and there's usually a limited choice under each heading. A certain amount of beer or wine is often included in the overall price.

Spanish mealtimes
In Spain, lunch and evening meals are much later than in Britain. Spaniards like to start lunch some time after two, and it can go on till four or later. So it's not surprising that some take an afternoon siesta. Evening meals tend to be eaten late – as late as 10 or 11pm.

Breakfast is usually light and happens at a more familiar time – about eight o'clock. In hotels, from eight till ten.

This time-table is however changing and the lunch hour is tending to get shorter and earlier, specially in the big cities. And now that Spain has joined the EEC it may change even more.

EATING OUT 2

RACIÓN 15

WHEN IN SPAIN ...
There are no set rules of course, but usually a full meal in Spain will consist of a starter (soup, hors d'oeuvres, shellfish, pasta, etc), a main course of fish, poultry or meat served with vegetables, and a sweet.
- To order, just name what you want:

de primero, sopa de verdura (for starters, vegetable soup)
de segundo, merluza (for the main course, hake)
de postre, flan (for sweet, creme caramel).
- One question the waiter will always ask is **¿Para beber?** (What will you have to drink?)
- When you're ready for the bill, you say:

La cuenta, por favor.

Costa del Sol – sunshine, shade and an aperitif

ACTION

Miguel goes for a meal in a restaurant, and has melon and ham, followed by lamb chops, with white wine. He doesn't have a dessert, but has a brandy with his coffee.

Miguel **Buenas noches.**
Waiter **Buenas noches, señor.**
Miguel **¿Qué tiene para comer?**
Waiter **Eh, pues tenemos melón con jamón, judías con jamón, sopa ...**
Miguel **¿Me pone melón con jamón, por favor?**
Waiter **Muy bien, señor ...**
Miguel **Y de segundo, ¿qué hay?**
Waiter **Pues mire usted, tenemos pollo con almendra, conejo con champiñón, entrecot, y ...**
Miguel **¿Tiene usted chuletas de cordero?**
Waiter **Sí, señor.**
Miguel **Eh, ¿me pone chuletas de cordero con patatas fritas, por favor?**
Waiter **Muy bien ... ¿para beber, señor?**
Miguel **Un vino blanco.**
Waiter **¿De la casa?**
Miguel **Sí, de la casa, por favor.**
Waiter **Muy bien ...** (After the main course) **¿Todo bien, señor?**
Miguel **Sí, sí, todo bien, gracias ...**
Waiter **¿Quiere algo de postre?**
Miguel **No, gracias, no quiero nada.**
Waiter **Pues, nada. ¿Café?**
Miguel **Sí, tráigame un café y una copa de coñac, por favor ...**
(at the end of the meal)
Miguel **¡Oiga! la cuenta, por favor.**
Waiter **En seguida, señor.**

REPLAY

1 The main thing you need for eating in a restaurant is to be able to recognise the items you are likely to find on the menu. You'll find many of them on page 80, note 6.

2 **¿Qué tiene para comer?** (What do you have to eat?) is one way of getting started. If the waiter speaks first, he's likely to say: **¿Qué va(n) a tomar?** (What will you have?)

3 Two slightly different ways of saying what you'd like: **¿Me pone chuletas?** (Can I have chops?) and **Quiero chuktas** (I want chops). 'I don't want anything' is: **No quiero nada.**

4 The waiter also had a question about wants: **¿Quiere algo de postre?** (Do you want something for dessert?)

5 **Oiga** is a very useful and polite way of attracting someone's attention, in a restaurant or anywhere else. It's often followed in a restaurant by **¡La cuenta, por favor!**

TRYOUT

You take a non-Spanish-speaking friend to a restaurant, so you have to do the ordering:

1 For the first course, you decide on fish soup, your friend wants a mixed salad.

2 Roast chicken to follow for you, pork chops and chips for your friend.

3 You decide on a bottle of red wine between you, and a bottle of still mineral water.

4 And for dessert, a creme caramel and fresh fruit.

5 Ask for two coffees – one black, one (large) white, and ask for the bill at the same time.

QUIZ

1 *Fawlty menus* You-know-who has made a mess of the menus again: a nice selection of dishes, but not quite under the right headings! Can you sort and write them out in 3 minutes?

Mariscos	*Verduras*	*Pescado*	*Carne*	*Postre*
merluza	cerdo	judías	flan	solomillo
guisantes	champiñones	besugo	lenguado	ternera
helado	almejas	fruta	mejillones	bistec

2 *Finish your drinks* The person ordering the drinks isn't sure about one or two words. Can you help by filling in the missing word in each drinks order? The dashes will help you (one per letter).

a **Dos vasos de vino** b l a n c o.
b **Un café** s o l o.
c **Una** b o t e l l a **de agua mineral.**
d **¿Con gas? No** sin gas.

Restaurants

Restaurants are classified by a fork symbol – five forks for a centre of gastronomic excellence, one fork for something fairly modest. But excellent meals can be had in the simplest one fork surroundings and you'll find that Spanish waiters are skilled and friendly.

Finding your way round a Spanish menu

It's difficult to predict what dishes will appear on any particular menu. But become familiar with the following headings and at least you can be sure you're not looking at the soups when you want a sweet.

sopas	soups
entremeses	hors d'oeuvres
pescados	fish
(y mariscos)	(and seafood)
aves	poultry
carnes	meats
verduras	vegetables
postres	sweets

Spanish food

You can expect to find the very best ingredients – salads in particular contain delicious lettuce and tomatoes. There's good quality meat, but it's the fish and seafood which are really outstanding. Even hundreds of miles inland the fish is very fresh.

Three famous Spanish dishes

Gazpacho
comes from Andalucía in the South. It's a soup served cold and made from olive oil, vinegar, tomatoes and garlic. Served with all sorts of garnishes, it's a delicious summer starter.

Paella
comes from Valencia on the East coast. It's made from saffron rice and seafood – shrimps, mussels, clams ... the possibilities are endless – and/or morsels of chicken and meat. Colour and vegetables are supplied by red pimentoes and green peas. It is cooked in a shallow iron pan. The very best paellas are made to order, and 'to measure' – so if you want one for lunch you should order it after breakfast ... and for so many people.

The paella man

Tortilla Española
Una tortilla is 'an omelette' and comes with the usual fillings (...*de queso, de jamón, de gambas* etc). However, a true *tortilla española* is not what we call 'Spanish omelette' (ie peppers and mixed vegetables). It is a large omelette with potatoes and onions, made with many eggs and cooked until firm. It is mostly eaten cold.

GRAMMAR WITH 'L' PLATES

Contents
1 'A' and 'THE'; choose your article carefully
2 AGREEMENT: and other ways of getting on in Spanish
3 VERBS: a happy ending
4 'HE', 'SHE' and 'IT': a major omission
5 'YOU'; a very special person
6 ASKING QUESTIONS: the way to get an answer
7 POSSESSION: nine-tenths of the law.

These notes don't aim to make you a grammar 'buff'. They try to explain briefly how the language works. Use them
a To check a point you're not sure of.
b When the *raciones* suggest you check a point.

1 'A' and 'The':
In Spanish there are two words for 'a' and four for 'the'. Why? Because
a In Spanish each word is either masculine or feminine. For example, the word *tapa* (a bar snack) is feminine, but *vaso* (glass) is masculine. This 'gender' affects the word you use for 'a' and 'the'.
b With 'the', you also have to consider whether the word it goes with is *single* or *plural* – that is, if there is one of them, or more. This will affect your choice of word for 'the'.

'A'

Una *tapa*   (feminine)
Un   *vaso*   (masculine)

'The'

El   *banco*   The bank   (masculine, singular)
La   *plaza*   The square   (feminine, singular)
Los *plátanos* The bananas (masculine, plural)
Las *peras*   The pears   (feminine, plural)

Suggestion: As you learn words, try to learn the word for 'a' or 'the' that goes with them.

2 Agreement:

Words that describe things or people, such as 'good' or 'small' (they're called adjectives) have variable endings. It all depends on what they are describing. Some examples should give you the idea:

Un melón **pequeño**	A small melon
Una cerveza **pequeña**	A small beer
Dos melones **pequeños**	Two small melons
Dos peras **pequeñas**	Two small pears
Un melón **grande**	A large melon
Una cerveza **grande**	A large beer
Dos melones **grandes**	Two large melons
Dos cervezas **grandes**	Two large beers

Suggestion: When you use a word which describes things or persons (an adjective), check that it looks and sounds like the end of the word it describes – as far as possible.

3 Verbs:

Verbs (words that usually show action) have a greater variety of endings in Spanish than in English:

Yo vivo *en Sleaford.*	**I live** in Sleaford.
¿Dónde **vive (usted)?**	Where do **you live?**
¿Dónde **vives (tú)?**	*or* (see note 5)
Soy *de York.*	**I'm** from York.
¿De dónde **es usted?**	*Where* **are you** *from?*

Suggestion: Most sentences have a verb; when you use a phrase, try to check that you are using the ending you learnt with the phrase.

4 'He', 'She' and 'It':

In Spanish the words for 'I', 'he' etc (pronouns) are often missed out, especially once you've established who you're talking about. This is because the ending of the verb (see 3 above) is sufficient to show who you're talking about and so 'I' 'you' 'she' etc. aren't necessary any more. *¿Cómo se llama usted, y de dónde es?* – What is your name and where are (you) from?.

Suggestions: If in doubt, use the pronoun – it may seem a bit awkward, but it's never wrong.

5 'You': a very special person.

In English you can call anyone 'You' – your baby daughter, the next door neighbour, or a County Court judge. But in Spanish, there is more than one word for 'you'. The choice depends on the person you are speaking to. 'What is your name', for example, can be:

*¿Cómo te llam**as** (tú)?* (to a young person or friend)
*¿Cómo se llam**a** (usted)?* (to an older person or stranger)

Notice the change in the ending of the verb. Generally speaking, if you call someone *tú* you add on an 's' to the end of the verb

usted habla – tú hablas (you speak)
usted vive – tú vives (you live)

An exception: *usted es – tú eres* (you are)

When you are talking to more than one person there are two more words *(vosotros/as, ustedes)*, each with different verb endings. But these can wait for a while!

Suggestion: Remember who you're speaking to! Try to use the same word as they use to you.

6 Asking questions:

Usted habla español (You speak Spanish) is a statement. To make it into a question (Do you speak Spanish?), you can:

Say the same thing with a question in your voice: *¿Usted habla español?*

Turn two words round: *¿Habla usted español?*

Do the same thing, but miss out the *usted*: *¿Habla español?*

Often questions begin with a question **word,** as in these examples:

¿Dónde *vive usted?* **Where** do you live?

¿Cuánto *valen las uvas?* **How much** are the grapes?

¿Cómo *se llama?* **What's** your name? (**How** are you called?')

7 Possession:

In English we often use the apostrophe 's' to show who something belongs to. For example:

Teresa is Sara's sister.

In Spanish there is no apostrophe 's', so we have to change the expression round, to say:

'Teresa is the sister of Sara.' *Teresa es la hermana* **de** *Sara.*

USEFUL WORDS

List of topics
1 – Drinks/Bebidas
2 – Appetizers and sandwiches/Tapas y bocadillos
3 – Food/Comestibles
4 – Places and shops/Establecimientos y tiendas
5 – Countries and nationalities/Países y nacionalidades
6 – Restaurant/Restaurante
7 – House and hotel/Casa y hotel
8 – Numbers and money/Números y dinero
9 – Weather/El tiempo
10 – Time/La hora
11 – Weights and measures/Pesos y medidas
12 – Clothes/Ropa
13 – The body/El cuerpo
14 – Presents/Regalos
15 – The car/El coche
16 – Professions/Profesiones

1 Drinks/Bebidas
- un refresco – a cool drink
- un zumo de fruta – a fruit juice; naranja – orange; piña – pineapple; tomate – tomato; limón – lemon
- una naranjada – an orange drink
- una limonada – a lemon drink
- una gaseosa – a fizzy lemonade
- un agua mineral con gas – a fizzy mineral water
- un agua mineral sin gas/natural – a still mineral water
- una cerveza – a (bottled) beer
- una caña – a draught beer
- una sidra – a cider
- un (vaso de) vino tinto – a (glass of) red wine
- un (vaso de) vino blanco – a (glass of) white wine
- un jerez (seco/dulce) – a sherry (dry/sweet)
- un champán – a champagne
- un vermút – a vermouth
- una ginebra – a gin

un coñac – a brandy
un anís – an anis (aniseed liqueur)
un cubalibre – a rum (or other spirit) and coke
una coca cola – a coke
un café (solo) – a (black) coffee
un café con leche – a large white coffee
un café cortado – a small white coffee
un té (con limón) – a (lemon) tea
un té con leche – a tea with milk
una leche fría – a cold milk
un chocolate caliente/frío – a hot/cold chocolate
una horchata – a cool drink made from nut juice
un batido – a milk shake

2 Appetizers and sandwiches/Tapas y bocadillos

una tapa – an appetizer
una ración – a portion
un bocadillo – a sandwich (made with a roll)
un sandwich – a toasted sandwich
un bocadillo de jamón – a ham sandwich
    patatas a la brava – chips with chili sauce
    sardinas – sardines
    anchoas – anchovies
    boquerones – (another sort of) anchovies
    almejas – clams
    aceitunas – olives
    jamón de York – York ham
    tortilla – omelette
    salchichón – salami
    chorizo – garlic sausage
    patatas fritas – crisps
    ensaladilla rusa – Russian salad
    pinchos morunos – small kebab on skewer
    churros – fried fingers of flavoured batter

3 Food/Comestibles

(see also section 6)
el pan – bread
la leche – milk
la carne – meat
los huevos – eggs
la fruta – fruit
una manzana – an apple

una naranja – an orange
una pera – a pear
un melón – a melon
una sandía – a water melon
un melocotón – a peach
una cereza – a cherry
un plátano – a banana
el salchichón – salami-type sausage
el chorizo – spicy sausage

4 Places and shops/Establecimientos y tiendas
la Oficina de Turismo – the Tourist Office
una agencia de viajes – a travel agent's
un hotel – an hotel
una pensión – a boarding house
un banco – a bank
la catedral – the cathedral
la iglesia – the church
el mercado – the market
   Correos – the Post office
la Plaza mayor – the Main Square
la estación (del ferrocarril) – the (railway) station
la estación del autobús – the bus station
el aeropuerto – the airport
el pub – smart bar/nightclub
la discoteca – the discotheque
una parada del autobús – a bus-stop
el castillo – the castle
el puerto – the port
la playa – the beach
un estanco – a tobacconist's, stamp seller's
una farmacia – a chemist's shop
una zapatería – a shoe-shop
unos almacenes – a department-store
un supermercado – a supermarket
una tienda de ultramarinos/comestibles – a grocer's
una frutería – a fruit shop
una panadería – a bread shop
una peluquería – a hairdresser's
una pastelería – a cake shop
un quiosco – a newspaper stall
los servicios – toilets

5 Countries and nationalities/Países y nacionalidades

Inglaterra, inglés – England, English
Escocia, escocés – Scotland, Scottish
Gales, galés – Wales, Welsh
Irlanda, irlandés – Ireland, Irish
Gran Bretaña, británico – Great Britain, British
España, español – Spain, Spanish
Portugal, portugués – Portugal, Portuguese
Francia, francés – France, French
Bélgica, belga – Belgium, Belgian
Holanda, holandés – Holland, Dutch
Suiza, suizo – Switzerland, Swiss
Alemania, alemán – Germany, German
Austria, austriaco – Austria, Austrian
Suecia, sueco – Sweden, Swedish
Italia, italiano – Italy, Italian

6 Restaurant/Restaurante

(see also Sections 1, 2 and 3)

   el desayuno – breakfast
   la comida – lunch
   la cena – dinner, supper
  un plato – a dish, a course
   el menú, la carta – the menu
   el menú del día – the set menu
 las entradas – entrées, starters
 los entremeses – hors d'oeuvres
   la sopa – soup
   el gazpacho – cold tomato-based soup
   la sopa de pescado – fish soup
   el consomé – clear soup, consommé
 los huevos al plato – fried eggs
   la tortilla (española) – (Spanish) omelette
   la tortilla francesa – plain omelette
   la ensalada (mixta) – (mixed) salad
   el arroz – rice
   la paella – paella
 los mariscos – seafood
   el pescado – fish
   la merluza – hake

el besugo – sea-bream
el lenguado – sole
el bacalao – cod
la trucha – trout
la carne – meat
la chuleta de cordero/cerdo – lamb/pork chop
el bistec – steak
el cordero – lamb
el escalope de ternera – veal escalope
el pollo asado – roast chicken
el lomo de cerdo – loin of pork
el entrecot – entrecote
el solomillo – fillet steak
el conejo – rabbit
las verduras – vegetables
las judías verdes – green beans
las habas – broad beans
los espárragos – asparagus
las patatas fritas – chips
las alcachofas – artichokes
los champiñones – mushrooms
el postre – dessert
el flan – caramel cream
el queso – cheese
el helado – ice cream
el membrillo – quince jelly
la fruta del tiempo – fresh fruit
la macedonia – fruit salad

7 House and hotel/Casa y hotel

una habitación individual/doble – a single/double room
el comedor – the dining room
el cuarto de baño – the bathroom
la bañera – the bath
la ducha – the shower
el váter – the toilet
el cuarto de estar/el salón – the sitting room/lounge
la cocina – the kitchen
el televisor – the television set
el teléfono – the telephone
una silla – a chair
una mesa – a table

8 Numbers and money/Números y dinero

1 uno	15 quince	28 veintiocho
2 dos	16 dieciséis	29 veintinueve
3 tres	17 diecisiete	30 treinta
4 cuatro	18 dieciocho	31 treinta y uno
5 cinco	19 diecinueve	32 treinta y dos
6 seis	20 veinte	33 treinta y tres
7 siete	21 veintiuno	40 cuarenta
8 ocho	22 veintidós	50 cincuenta
9 nueve	23 veintitrés	60 sesenta
10 diez	24 veinticuatro	70 setenta
11 once	25 veinticinco	80 ochenta
12 doce	26 veintiséis	90 noventa
13 trece	27 veintisiete	100 cien
14 catorce		

106 ciento seis
117 ciento diecisiete
158 ciento cincuenta y ocho
200 doscientos
300 trescientos
400 cuatrocientos
500 quinientos
600 seiscientos
700 setecientos
800 ochocientos
900 novecientos
1000 mil

una peseta
cinco pesetas ('un duro')
veinticinco pesetas
cincuenta pesetas
cien pesetas
quinientas pesetas
mil pesetas
cinco mil pesetas

primero, segundo, tercero – 1st, 2nd, 3rd

9 Weather/El tiempo

¿Qué tiempo hace?	What's the weather like?
Hace buen tiempo	It's nice
Hace mal tiempo	The weather's bad
Hace calor	It's warm
Hace frío	It's cold
Hace sol	It's sunny
Hace viento	It's windy
Está lloviendo	It's raining
Está nevando	It's snowing
Está nublado	It's cloudy
Llueve en invierno	It rains in winter

10 Time/La hora

¿Qué hora es? – What's the time?

 1.00 Es la una – it's 1 o'clock
 2.00 Son las dos – it's 2 o'clock
 3.00 Son las tres – it's 3 o'clock
12.00 Son las doce – it's 12 o'clock
12.00 Es mediodía – it's midday
12.00 Es medianoche – it's midnight
 4.30 Son las cuatro y media – it's 4.30
 5.15 Son las cinco y cuarto – it's 5.15
 6.20 Son las seis y veinte – it's 6.20
 7.45 Son las ocho menos cuarto – it's 7.45
 8.50 Son las nueve menos diez – it's 8.50
11.00 Son las once de la mañana – it's 11.00 in the morning
11.00 Son las once de la noche – it's 11.00 at night
 3.00 Son las tres de la tarde – it's 3.00 in the afternoon

11 Weights & measures/Pesos y medidas

- 1kg un kilo
- ½kg medio kilo
- 2kg dos kilos
- 500g quinientos gramos
- 250g doscientos cincuenta gramos
- 100g cien gramos

- 1l un litro
- ½ l medio litro

- 1m un metro
- 10cm diez centímetros
- 3mm tres milímetros
- 1km un kilómetro
- 100km cien kilómetros

12 Clothes/Ropa

- la ropa – clothes
- un sombrero – a hat
- un abrigo – an overcoat
- una chaqueta – a jacket
- un traje – a suit
- unas botas – boots

una	blusa	– a blouse
una	falda	– a skirt
un	vestido	– a dress
unas	bragas	– a pair of pants
unas	medias	– stockings
un	jersey	– a jumper
un	cinturón	– a belt
una	camisa	– a shirt
una	corbata	– a tie
un	pantalón	– a pair of trousers
un	pantalón vaquero	– a pair of jeans
unos	calzoncillos	– underpants
unos	zapatos	– shoes
unos	calcetines	– socks
un	traje de baño	– bathing costume
unas	gafas de sol	– sunglasses
el	bikini	– bikini

13 The human body/El cuerpo

la	cabeza	– the head
la	cara	– the face
el	pelo	– the hair
los	ojos	– the eyes
la	nariz	– the nose
las	orejas	– the ears
la	espalda	– the back
la	boca	– the mouth
los	dientes	– the teeth
las	muelas	– the back teeth
el	cuello	– the neck
el	pecho	– the chest
el	estómago	– the stomach
la	cintura	– the waist
los	brazos	– the arms
las	manos	– the hands
los	dedos	– the fingers
el	pulgar	– the thumb
las	piernas	– the legs
los	pies	– the feet
los	dedos del pie	– the toes
las	quemaduras de sol	– sunburn

14 Presents/Regalos

- un monedero – a purse
- el perfume – perfume
- el after-shave – after shave
- un reloj – a watch
- un bolso – a handbag
- unos guantes – gloves
- la cerámica – pottery
- un pañuelo – a handkerchief
- una guitarra – a guitar
- unas castañuelas – castanets
- el jabón – soap
- la joyería – jewellery
- unos pendientes – earrings
- un collar – a necklace
- una pulsera – a bracelet
- un porrón – a wine container (poured from above head)
- una bota de vino – a wineskin
- un botijo – a drinking jug
- un abanico – a fan
- un mechero – a cigarette lighter
- una muñeca – a doll

15 The car/El coche

- el volante – the steering wheel
- los frenos – the brakes
- el embrague – the clutch
- el parabrisas – the windscreen
- los faros – the headlights
- las luces oscilantes – the indicators
- el aceite – oil
- la gasolina – petrol
- la rueda – the wheel
- el neumático – the tyre
- un pinchazo – a puncture
- una avería – a breakdown
- las obras – road works
- un accidente – accident
- el semáforo – traffic lights
- dirección única – one-way
- prohibido – prohibited

16 Professions/Profesiones

- el ama de casa – housewife
- el panadero – the baker
- el relojero – the watchmaker
- el médico – the doctor
- el/la dentista – the dentist
- la enfermera – the nurse
- el/la recepcionista – the receptionist
- el mecánico – the mechanic
- el técnico – the technician
- el obrero – workman
- el operario – machine operator
- la secretaria – the secretary
- el ingeniero – the engineer
- el electricista – the electrician
- el fontanero – the plumber
- el albañil – the builder
- el carpintero – the carpenter
- el dependiente/la dependienta – the shop assistant
- el director – the manager
- el labrador – the farm worker
- el taxista – the taxi driver
- el camionero – the lorry driver
- el hombre de negocios – the businessman
- el/la estudiante – the student
- jubilado/jubilada – retired
- desempleado/desempleada – unemployed

ANSWERS

Ración 1
Tryout
1 Buenas tardes. Una caña (de cerveza) por favor
2 Buenos días. Un café (sólo) y un café con leche por favor
3 Un vaso de vino blanco y un whisky con hielo por favor
4 Una copa de coñac y un café cortado por favor

Quiz
1 Caña; copa; café; vino
2 Cerveza

Ración 2
Tryout
1 Un plano de Benidorm por favor
2 Un sello para Inglaterra por favor
3 Un sello para Francia por favor
4 70 pesetas

Quiz
1 10 (diez)
2 postal; plano; sello
3 Inglaterra; España; Irlanda; Gales; Francia

Ración 3
Tryout
1 Me llamo (+ your name)
2 ¿Cómo se llama (usted)?
3 ¿Cómo te llamas?
4 ¿De dónde es (usted)?
5 (a) Spain (woman) (b) Wales (woman)
   (c) Ireland (man) (d) France (man)

Quiz
1 (a) ¿Cómo te llamas?
   (b) Me llamo Isabel, ¿y tú?
   (c) ¿Es usted inglesa? No, soy escocesa
2 (a) usted (b) llamo (c) ¿cómo?
3 (a) llamas (b) usted (c) soy

Ración 4

Tryout

1 ¿Habla usted inglés?
2 Sí, hablo un poquito
3 ¿Hablas (tú) inglés?
4 (i) Hablo inglés pero soy escocés (or escocesa)
(ii) Soy inglés (or inglesa) y hablo un poquito el español
(iii) Soy galés (or galesa) y hablo inglés y galés

Quiz

1 Hablo; hablas; habla
2 ¿Habla usted inglés? (Do you speak English?)
Hablo un poco el español (I speak Spanish a bit)
3 The answer is 'no'. Inglés, escocés, galés are possible; irlandés is not.
4 El italiano; el alemán; el francés.

Ración 5

Tryout

1 ¿La Oficina de Turismo por favor?
2 ¿Dónde está el Hotel Esmeralda por favor?
3 ¿(Dónde está) Correos, por favor?
4 Straight ahead and to the left

Quiz

1 Izquierda (derecha and todo recto ok)
2 (a) iii;
 (b) iv;
 (c) ii;
 (d) i

Ración 6

Tryout

1 ¿Qué tapas tiene(n)?
2 Una ración de gambas y una de tortilla
3 Un vaso de vino tinto y una cerveza

Quiz

1 Buenas tardes. ¿Hay tapas?
Sí, hay gambas, tortilla y calamares
Dos raciones de tortilla y una de gambas por favor
2 (a) iv;   (c) i;
 (b) iii;   (d) ii

Ración 7

Tryout

1 Buenos días. Un poco de queso por favor
2 Doscientos gramos de jamón serrano
3 No, nada más
4 ¿Cuánto es?
5 380 pesetas

Quiz

1 Queso; chorizo; jamón; vino; salchichón
2 (a) aquí tiene (b) ¿me da …? (c) ¿algo más? (d) nada más (e) ¿cuánto es?
3 (a) ii; (b) v; (c) i; (d) iv; (e) iii

Ración 8

Tryout

1 ¿Cuánto vale esta camisa?
2 Yes. It costs 4,450 pesetas
3 Vale (or muy bien)
4 ¿Cuánto valen estos zapatos?
5 635 pesetas
6 Muchas gracias
7 ¿Cuánto vale esto?

Quiz

1 (a) iv; (b) i; (c) v; (d) iii; (e) ii
2 ¿Cuánto valen éstas?

Ración 9

Tryout

1 ¿Tiene una habitación doble?
2 Con ducha
3 Para dos noches
4 Give him/her your passport
5 Room 138

Quiz

1 La habitación número ochocientos siete (Room 807)
2 (i) Novecientos
 (ii) baño
 (iii) individual
 (iv) ducha

Ración 10

Tryout

1 Buenas tardes ¿Qué bocadillos tiene(n)?
2 Un bocadillo de queso y uno de tortilla
3 Un zumo de naranja y una cerveza
4 Un helado de pistacho y uno de vainilla
5 Cincuenta pesetas de churros por favor

Quiz

1 Un bocadillo de tortilla por favor
   ¿Me da cincuenta pesetas de churros?
2 (a) bocadillo (not a sandwich filling)
   (b) churro (not an ice-cream flavour)
   (c) zumo (you can't eat it)

Ración 11

Tryout

1 Me llamo (your name)
2 Soy de (your town)
3 ¿Y tú?
4 Seville
5 ¿En qué trabajas (tú)?
6 She's a rep for a plastics firm

Quiz

1 (a) española (b) escocesa (c) irlandés (d) galés (e) inglés
2 ¿Cómo te llamas? Me llamo Clara
   ¿De dónde eres? Soy de York
   ¿En que trabajas? Soy secretaria
3 Secretaria; empleado; profesora; dependiente

Ración 12

Tryout

1 Súper, por favor
2 Lleno, por favor
3 3,220 pesetas
4 ¿Donde están los servicios?
5 Over there on the right

Quiz

1 (a) normal (b) súper (c) servicios (d) mapas
2 (a) lleno (b) estación (c) litros (d) servicios
3 (a) por favor (b) buen viaje (c) ¿algo más?

Ración 13

Tryout

1 Dos billetes de ida y vuelta para Alicante por favor
2 1,780 pesetas
3 ¿A qué hora es el próximo?
4 ¿Hay autobuses para Calpe?
5 Un billete de ida (sólo) por favor.

Quiz

1 (a) billete (b) ida sólo
  (c) ida y vuelta (d) ¿a qué hora?

Ración 14

Tryout

1 Un vaso de vino blanco, un vaso de vino tinto, una ración de tortilla española, una de gambas, una de ensaladilla rusa y una de aceitunas
2 ¿Me da un poco de pan por favor?
3 ¿El número tres tiene huevos?
4 Un número tres y un número seis por favor

Quiz

1 Tortilla; aceitunas; anchoas; gambas, sepia; atún; almejas; pulpos
2 (a) cuatro del uno (b) tres del tres (c) uno del dos (d) dos del uno

Ración 15

Tryout

1 De primero, una sopa de pescado y una ensalada mixta
2 Un pollo asado y una chuleta de cerdo con patatas fritas
3 Una botella de vino tinto y una botella de agua mineral sin gas
4 De postre, un flan y una fruta
5 Un café (sólo) y un café con leche, y la cuenta por favor

Quiz

1 *Mariscos:* mejillones; almejas
  pescado: besugo; lenguado; merluza
  carne: cerdo; bistec; solomillo; ternera
  verduras: guisantes; champiñones; judías
  postre: flan; fruta; helado

2 (a) blanco (b) sólo (c) botella (d) sin gas

SPANISH-ENGLISH VOCABULARY

A
Acuerdo: de acuerdo OK
- el **agua** water
- **ahí** there; **por ahí** over there
- **ahora** now; **ahora mismo** right away
- **algo** something; **¿algo más?** anything else?
- **allí** there; **por allí** over there
- la **almeja** clam
- la **almendra** almond
- **aquí** here; **aquí tiene** here you are
- el **árabe** Arabic
- **asado** roast
- **así** like this
- el **autobús** bus

B
- el **baño** bath
- el **barril** barrel
- el **batido** milkshake
- **beber** to drink; **¿para beber?** What would you like to drink?
- el **beicon** bacon
- el **besugo** bream
- **bien** well
- el **bikini** bikini
- el **billete** ticket
- el **bistec** steak
- **blanco-a** white
- el **bocadillo** sandwich
- la **bota de vino** wineskin
- **bueno-a** good; **¡buen viaje!** have a good trip!

C
- el **café** coffee; **café sólo** black coffee; **café con leche** white coffee; **café cortado** strong white coffee
- el **calamar** squid
- la **caña** glass of draught beer
- la **carretera** road
- la **casa** house
- **casado-a** married
- el **centro** centre
- el **cerdo** pork
- la **cereza** cherry
- la **cerveza** beer
- la **cebolla** onion
- la **ciudad** city/town
- **claro** of course
- **comer** to eat
- **¿cómo?** what? how?; **¿cómo se llama?** what's your name?
- **comprar** to buy
- **con** with; **con gas** fizzy
- el **coñac** brandy
- el **conejo** rabbit
- la **copa** glass (for or of brandy)
- el **cordero** lamb
- **Correos** Post Office
- **¿cuál?** which one?
- **¿cuanto-a?** how much?; **¿cuánto es?** how much does it come to?; **¿cuánto vale(n)?** how much is it? (are they?); **¿cuántos-as?** how many?
- la **cuenta** bill

CH

- el **chorizo** spicy sausage
- el **chocolate** chocolate
- el **churro** deep fried batter
- la **chuleta** chop
- el **champiñón** mushroom

D

- **da; ¿me da..?** Can I have..?
- **de** of, from; **de acuerdo** OK
- la **derecha** right
- **desea; ¿qué desea?** What would you like?
- **detrás** behind
- **¿dónde?** Where?
- la **ducha** shower
- **dura** it lasts

E

- **entonces** then
- el **entrecot** sirloin steak
- **eres** you are
- **es** it is, he is, she is, you are
- **español-a** Spanish
- **está** it is, he is, she is, you are
- la **estación** station
- el **estanco** tobacconist's
- **este, esta** this
- la **estrachatela** stracciatela
- **esto** this
- **estos, estas** these

F

- **favor; por favor** please
- el **flan** crème caramel
- **fondo: al fondo** at the back
- **francés-francesa** French
- la **fresa** strawberry
- **frito** fried
- la **fruta** fruit

G

- la **gamba** prawn
- el **gas** gas; **con gas** fizzy; **sin gas** still
- la **gasolina** petrol
- el **gramo** gram
- el **guisante** pea

H

- la **habitación** room
- **habla: ¿habla usted?** do you speak?
- **hablo** I speak; **no hablo** I don't speak
- **hay** there is, there are; **no hay de qué** don't mention it
- el **helado** ice cream
- la **hermana** sister
- el **hermano** brother
- el **hielo** ice
- el **horario** timetable
- **hoy** today
- el **huevo** egg

I

- **ida; de ida sólo** single (ticket); **de ida y vuelta** return
- el **idioma** language
- **individual** single (room)
- **inglés-inglesa** English
- **irlandés-irlandesa** Irish
- la **izquierda** left

J

- el **jamón** ham; **jamón serrano** naturally cured ham
- la **judía** green bean

K

- el **kilo** kilo

L

- la **leche** milk
- el **lenguado** Dover sole
- **libre** free
- el **limón** lemon

- el **litro** litre
- la **lonja** slice

LL
- **llama: se llama** he's called, she's called ¿**cómo se llama usted?** What's your name?
- **llamo: me llamo** my name is
- **llamas: ¿Cómo te llamas?** What's your name?
- **lleno** full tank

M
- **mañana** tomorrow
- el **mapa** map
- los **mariscos** seafood
- **más** more; ¿**algo más?** anything else? **nada más** nothing else
- el **mejillón** mussel
- el **melón** melon
- el **menú** menu, set meal
- la **merienda** picnic
- la **merluza** hake
- **mineral** mineral
- el **minuto** minute
- ¡**mire!** look!
- el **momento** moment
- **muy** very

N
- **nada** nothing; **nada más** nothing else; **de nada** don't mention it
- la **naranja** orange
- el **niño** child
- **no** no; **no hablo** I don't speak
- la **noche** night
- el **número** number

O
- la **oficina** office
- ¡**oiga!** excuse me!
- **otro-a** another (one)

P
- el **país** country, region
- el **pan** bread
- **para** for
- la **parada** stop
- el **pasaporte** passport
- la **patata** potato
- **pero** but
- **perfecto** perfect
- la **persona** person
- el **pescado** fish
- la **plancha** grill
- el **plano** street plan
- el **plato** dish; **plato combinado** set dish
- el **pollo** chicken
- **pone;** ¿**me pone..?** Will you give me..?
- un **poquito** just a bit
- **por** for; **por favor** please; **por allí** over there; **por supuesto** of course
- la **postal** postcard
- el **postre** dessert
- **primero** first; **de primero** for starters
- el **profesor/la profesora** teacher
- **próximo** next (one)

Q
- **que** which
- ¿**qué?** what?; **no hay de qué** don't mention it
- el **queso** cheese
- **quiero** I want

R
- la **ración** portion
- la **región** region
- la **reserva/la reservación** reservation
- **romana; a la romana** deep-fried in batter
- **rosado** rosé

S

- la **secretaria** secretary
- **seguida: en seguida** straight away
- **segundo-a** second; **de segundo** for the main course
- el **sello** stamp
- la **sepia** cuttlefish
- los **servicios** toilets
- **sólo** only; **café sólo** black coffee
- el **solomillo** fillet steak
- **soltero-a** single (unmarried)
- la **sopa** soup
- **soy** I am
- el **súper** 4 star petrol

T

- la **tapa** appetizer
- el **taxi** taxi
- **tenemos** we have
- la **ternera** veal
- el **tiempo** time
- la **tienda** shop
- **tiene** you have; **¿tiene?** have you got?
- **tienen** you have; **¿tienen?** have you got?
- **todo-a** all; **todo recto** straight on
- **¡tome!** here you are!
- la **tortilla** omelette
- el **total** total
- **trabaja: ¿en qué trabaja (usted)?** What work do you do?
- **tráigame** bring me
- el **tren** train
- **tú** you
- el **turismo** tourism; tourist office
- el **turrón** nougat

U

- el **único** only one
- **usted** you

V

- la **vainilla** vanilla
- **vale** OK
- **valenciano-a** Valencian
- **verde** green
- la **verdura** vegetables
- el **vino** wine

Y

- **y** and

Z

- el **zapato** shoe
- el **zumo** juice

La Sagrada Familia in Barcelona – Gaudi's greatest creation

San Sebastian – the Spanish fishing fleet is one of the largest in Europe